MOMENTUM TRADING

Master The Wave and Volume Edge For Consistent Profits

Frank Miller

TABLE OF CONTENTS

INTRODUCTION

Most traders spend years chasing the same thing without ever naming it clearly. They study candlestick patterns, map out market structure, track price swings across multiple timeframes, and layer indicator upon indicator onto their charts. Every day in the market, they watch the ongoing battle between the Bulls and the Bears — analyzing, adjusting, second-guessing. And yet, when it comes time to pull the trigger on a trade, uncertainty creeps in. The analysis looks right, but something feels off. The setup appears clean, but the trade falls apart almost immediately after entry.

The missing piece, more often than not, is momentum.

Not momentum in the abstract sense — but a precise, structured understanding of how price is moving and what is driving it at any given moment. Pause for a moment and ask yourself: what is the real purpose behind all the analysis you do each day? Behind every candlestick you study, every structural level you mark, every indicator you consult — what are you ultimately trying to determine?

The answer is simpler than most traders expect: you are trying to assess the market's momentum. You are trying to determine whether the current trend is still strong or already beginning to weaken.

Whether you are reading the broader picture of the market or zooming in on smaller pieces — individual price swings, candlestick formations, support and resistance levels — the essence of the analysis revolves around a single core question: how is price momentum evolving? Is the current bullish or bearish move still supported by active capital flow? Or are there early signs that the side currently in control is starting to lose strength?

Accurately evaluating momentum is what allows us to bridge the gap between the market's broader structure and the final step of the analytical process: the decision to enter a trade. Without it, even the best-looking setups carry far more risk than they appear to on the surface.

Originally, the concept of momentum was developed purely through price action — by observing price waves to judge whether a bullish or bearish move was still maintaining its strength. This approach remains just as relevant today and will continue to play an important role in the trading framework presented in this book. But as modern trading has evolved, we now have more ways to evaluate momentum. Instead of relying solely on price behavior, we can incorporate additional signals from the market to build a more complete and reliable picture.

Above all, the goal is to follow the footprints of smart money — the large flows of capital that have the power to shape market movements. When we understand what they are doing, we gain a significant advantage in anticipating the market's next move before it becomes obvious to the majority.

In this book, momentum will be analyzed alongside volume through the method known as Volume Spread Analysis, or VSA — an approach many of you may already be familiar with. Volume will appear throughout the trading examples in this book because it serves as an important voice that helps us better understand what is truly happening behind the price chart. Price can be ambiguous. Volume leaves footprints. Learning to read those footprints is one of the most powerful skills a trader can develop.

It is important to note that most analyses are presented within the context of an uptrend or an uptrend transitioning into a downtrend. To maintain clarity and avoid unnecessary repetition, the same principles are not explicitly restated for the opposite direction. However, all concepts can be applied equivalently in a downtrend by simply reversing the logic.

SMT — The Soul of This Book

The entire book is built around a tightly connected structure. Each part does not stand alone — instead, it supports and strengthens the previous one, gradually forming a complete trading framework.

As you move through the chapters, you will encounter familiar concepts, but viewed from a new perspective. Both old and new ideas will be refined, combined, and organized through a single unifying approach that will help you understand them more deeply, remember them more easily, and apply them more effectively in real trading situations.

That approach is SMT — **Structure, Momentum, Trigger**.

These are the three layers of market validation we work through before executing any trade. Each step represents a critical stage in the analytical process. If even one of these steps is missing, your decision-making becomes less reliable and far more vulnerable to market noise. Structure tells you where you are in the market. Momentum tells you what is happening beneath the surface. And the trigger tells you precisely when to act.

In this book, I will walk you step by step through how to analyze market structure, how to evaluate momentum with both price action and volume, and how to identify a high-quality trade trigger. You will learn how to read the overall strength of the market, recognize the signals that truly matter, and apply practical techniques that can significantly improve both the quality of your analysis and the consistency of your results.

One of the key strengths of the SMT framework is that it is not a closed or rigid system. You can integrate it with many other trading strategies without worrying about signal conflicts. The reason is straightforward: SMT is built entirely on the market's core elements — price action and volume — and does not rely on lagging indicators. It adapts naturally to different markets and timeframes, which means it remains useful regardless of how market conditions shift over time.

Who This Book Is Written For

This book is written for investors and traders who already have a basic understanding of technical analysis. Readers should be familiar with foundational concepts such as candlesticks, trends, support and resistance, and basic volume analysis. If you are completely new to trading, I would recommend building that foundation first before working through the material here.

This book does not promise a perfect winning formula or a holy grail for trading. What it does promise is a clear framework for evaluating momentum in a systematic way, a developed ability to read price waves and volume as guiding signals, and a structured trading process built on objective criteria rather than intuition or guesswork.

The Journey Ahead

After finishing this book, you may find that trading is not as complicated as many people make it out to be. In many cases, consistent success comes from doing the opposite of what most traders do — removing unnecessary noise, focusing on the key trading zones, and waiting patiently for high-quality signals to appear within those areas. Simplicity, applied with discipline, is a far more powerful edge than complexity ever will be.

This entire process will be explained step by step across the ten chapters of the book. And because the goal is to genuinely help you master these ideas rather than simply understand them in theory, a dedicated learning and practice roadmap is included at the end of the book. Think of it as a practical guide designed to help you gradually turn the concepts on these pages into real, applied trading skill.

A great deal of thought and effort has gone into every part of this book. I hope it gives you not just knowledge, but clarity — the kind of clarity that makes a real difference when you are sitting in front of your charts and the market is moving. Now let's begin.

CHAPTER 1: INTRODUCTION TO MOMENTUM TRADING

Welcome to the first chapter—where we begin our journey into the core ideas behind this book. Momentum is not a foreign or complicated concept for most traders. However, truly understanding momentum—and applying momentum trading effectively—requires a structured approach. You need a method that allows you to identify opportunities consistently while avoiding many of the common traps the market tends to set for traders.

Take a look at the two charts below. Both show clear uptrends in two different currency pairs. At first glance, they appear quite similar—both markets are moving upward. But if you focus only on price structure and ignore the message of momentum, you may miss an important signal that separates a strong trend from a weaker one.

Don't worry—I'm not diving deep into theory with these charts just yet. Their purpose is simply to give you an initial glimpse of the main theme of this book. As we move through the chapters, we will gradually explore the full framework in a clear and systematic way.

Figure 1.1: Chart Example

Figure 1.2: Chart Example

Figures 1.1 and 1.2 show the EUR/JPY and AUD/USD exchange rates on the 1-hour timeframe. At first glance, both charts display strong uptrends with very similar characteristics. In each case, the market forms short-term highs at points A and B. After these highs, price only pulls back slightly, suggesting that the selling pressure during the corrections is relatively weak. Buyers remain in control of the market even when price temporarily moves lower.

In the final candle of both examples, we see large bullish candles with noticeably long bodies. The size of these candle bodies reflects strong buying pressure from the bulls pushing the market upward with conviction. More importantly, the closing price of each candle has been above the previous short-term highs—point A in EUR/JPY chart and point B in AUD/USD chart.

In short, both charts appear to show very healthy bullish momentum. The structure is bullish. The price action looks strong. On the surface, both markets seem to present reliable uptrends.

However, the next two charts will reveal a completely different story.

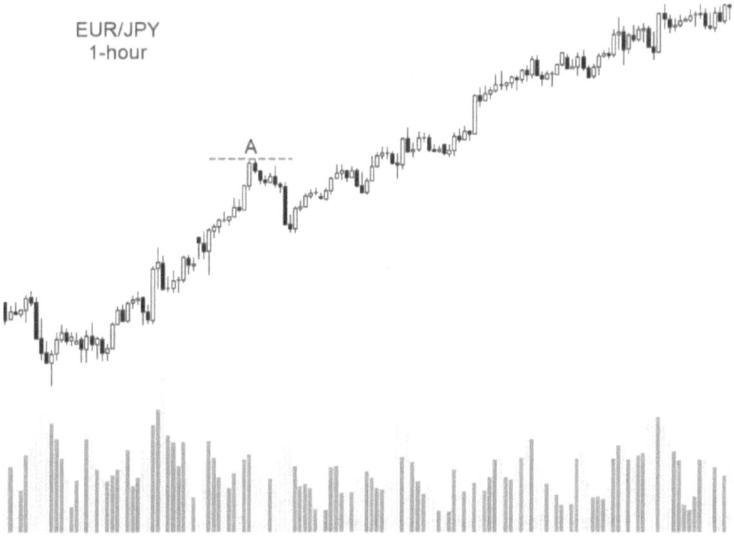

Figure 1.3: Chart Example

Figure 1.4: Chart Example

EUR/JPY Chart: After the breakout candle, price continues to climb strongly, moving well beyond the previous short-term high at point A. The uptrend maintains strong positive momentum.

AUD/USD Chart: Not long after the strong bullish candle we just discussed, price begins to weaken and gradually shifts into a clear downtrend. The market forms a sequence of lower lows and lower highs, signaling that the buyers are losing strength.

Both charts started from the same initial price structure, yet what followed could not be more different. One trend continues to rise with strength, while the other reverses and collapses.

This raises an important question: if you only looked at the price structure in Figures 1.1 and 1.2, would you have enough information to tell which trend was truly strong and which one was about to reverse? Is there a crucial element we might be overlooking?

The answer lies in **market momentum**.

When you combine price structure analysis with momentum analysis, the two charts no longer look the same. Momentum reveals the truth hidden behind the surface of price action. One chart shows that capital flow is still actively supporting the trend and pushing prices higher. The other suggests that smart money is quietly stepping away, leaving behind subtle warning signs.

For now, I won't go into the detailed momentum analysis of these two charts. I'll leave that exercise to you. Once you've mastered the techniques presented in this book, come back to these charts and see if you can uncover the answer yourself. At this stage, we are simply introducing the core concepts and building a basic foundation for the deeper analysis that will follow later in the book.

Traditional technical analysis tends to focus primarily on price structure—candlestick patterns, trendlines, and areas of support and resistance. These are valuable and essential tools, but they only tell half the story of what is happening in the market. The other half—often overlooked yet critical to the final outcome—is told by momentum.

Technical analysis in the stock market and other financial markets has evolved over decades, producing countless methods and tools. In this book, I propose a more integrated approach, where momentum is understood and evaluated through two complementary dimensions: price structure and volume behavior.

Price structure tells you where the market is moving. Volume behavior tells you whether that movement carries real conviction and strength.

Together, these two perspectives provide a much more complete picture of the true strength of a trend. They help you distinguish between price movements that are genuinely supported by capital flow and those that lack real backing—and are therefore far more likely to reverse.

Two Perspectives on Momentum

Momentum Through Wave Structure

This approach evaluates the strength of a trend by examining the structural characteristics of price movement. In essence, it focuses on three key elements:

The progression of impulse waves

Here, we measure the price distance between consecutive highs or lows. Is this distance expanding—suggesting accelerating momentum—or shrinking, which may indicate that the trend is losing strength?

The depth of corrective waves

This involves observing how deeply price pulls back after each impulsive move. Are the pullbacks becoming shallower, suggesting that the opposing side is weakening? Or are they growing deeper, signaling that the dominant trend may be losing control?

The slope and steepness of price waves

This element looks at how quickly price changes over time. Is the slope of the wave becoming steeper, indicating that the trend is gaining speed? Or is it flattening out, suggesting a loss of momentum?

This wave-structure approach provides a clear picture of the shape of a trend—how price moves through both space and time. In other words, it allows you to see a visual representation of momentum from a structural and geometric perspective.

However, this approach has an important limitation: it does not fully answer the question of where the movement comes from. You can observe the price movements, but you still don't know what is truly driving them beneath the surface. A trend may appear strong in its structure, yet still lack genuine conviction behind it.

Volume Spread Analysis (VSA)

The volume spread analysis (VSA) school approaches momentum from a different angle: the relationship between trading volume and the price spread of each bar. Instead of asking the question, "How is price moving?", VSA asks a deeper one: "Who is trading—and why are they trading at this particular moment?"

VSA is built on a simple but powerful principle: important price movements almost always leave clear traces in trading volume. Volume reflects the footprint of capital flow. When large institutional players actively buy or sell, trading volume tends to expand significantly, reflecting the intensity of their activity. In contrast, when the market is driven mostly by smaller retail positions without meaningful participation from smart money, the volume often lacks conviction. The volume signature in these situations is very different.

This distinction becomes especially important when comparing trends. Two trends may look very similar from a price-structure perspective—they may share the same pattern, the same sequence of higher highs and higher lows. But volume often reveals the hidden truth: which trend is supported by strong participation from smart money, and which one is merely a surface-level move with little real backing—making it far more vulnerable to reversal.

In that sense, VSA gives traders something like an X-ray view of the market, allowing them to see what is really happening beneath the surface of price action.

An Expanded Definition of Momentum

Based on an integrated approach that combines wave structure and volume analysis, this book proposes a broader and more comprehensive definition of momentum:

Momentum is the combined assessment of a trend's strength and sustainability, evaluated through two complementary dimensions.

(1) **Structural momentum** – This dimension measures the "shape" of the trend. It is reflected in the progression of impulse waves, the depth of corrective waves, and the slope or steepness of price movements. Structural momentum answers the question: "How is the trend moving?"

(2) **Volume momentum** – This dimension measures the "source" and the conviction behind the trend. It is reflected in how volume behaves during different phases of the trend—whether volume expands or contracts during impulse waves, how it changes during corrective waves, and how it behaves within the individual candles that form each wave. Volume momentum answers the question: "Who is behind this trend, and do they have real conviction?"

This definition does not treat the two elements as separate methods. Instead, they are viewed as two complementary sides of the same phenomenon. Wave structure shows you what the trend looks like. Volume reveals whether the trend has genuine substance behind it.

When you evaluate momentum through both of these dimensions, you begin to recognize many price behaviors that might otherwise appear ordinary but actually carry important warning signals. What looks similar on a price chart can reveal a very different story when viewed through the lens of integrated momentum analysis.

Momentum trading tends to work best when signals are confirmed by both components at the same time. A trend with strong wave structure but little volume support is fragile—and the opposite is equally true.

The SMT Framework

The trading approach presented in this book is built on three closely connected pillars, summarized by the acronym **SMT**:

S – Structure: This pillar identifies the current position of price within the broader market cycle, the direction of the main trend, and the key support and resistance zones where price is likely to react. Structure answers the question: *"Where are we in the bigger picture of the market?"*

M – Momentum: This pillar evaluates the true strength and sustainability of the ongoing trend. The assessment is based on both wave-structure analysis (wave progression, spacing, and slope) and volume behavior (levels of participation and conviction). Momentum answers the question: *"Is this trend strong enough to continue?"*

T – Trigger: This pillar focuses on identifying precise, high-probability entry points based on validated trading setups. A trigger is not an arbitrary entry; it is a specific setup that appears at the right moment within the context of structure and momentum. Trigger answers the question: *"When is the optimal moment to enter a trade?"*

This is exactly the structured framework I mentioned at the beginning of the book. Instead of chasing every price movement or reacting to every pattern that appears on the chart, you work with a systematic process for evaluating each trading opportunity. The framework forces you to ask the right questions before committing capital.

Momentum—with its expanded definition that includes both structure analysis and volume analysis—plays a central role in the SMT framework. It acts as the critical bridge between understanding the market's position (structure) and executing trades with precision (trigger). Without momentum confirmation, structure becomes little more than observation, and triggers become little more than speculation. Momentum transforms raw market information into actionable insight.

At this point, the chapter has introduced the core foundation of the book: **momentum**. Through the earlier examples, you have seen how two trends can appear nearly identical in terms of price structure, yet produce completely different outcomes afterward. That difference is not random—it reflects the footprint of smart money.

Before you can properly analyze momentum or identify high-quality triggers, you must first master the initial foundation: **structure**. You need to know how to read market structure accurately. In the next chapter, we will focus on building that skill. You will learn how to identify swing highs and swing lows using clear and systematic rules—from basic guidelines suitable for beginners to more advanced techniques for complex situations. You will also learn what truly defines a valid break, the early signs that may signal a potential reversal, and how to determine the overall market trend in just a few seconds.

CHAPTER 2: MARKET STRUCTURE

This chapter equips you with the skills to read market structure in a systematic and objective way. You will learn how to identify the pivot points that truly matter, distinguish meaningful structural swings from market noise, and recognize when a trend is continuing versus when the underlying structure is beginning to shift. These are foundational skills on which all later analysis will build.

The chapter is organized into four progressive sections. The first section introduces how to identify valid swings using the five-candle rule and how to handle more complex variations. The second section focuses on identifying swing highs and swing lows that carry real structural significance. The third section explains how to recognize market reversals, using two essential conditions designed to filter out false breaks. The fourth section shows how to quickly assess the dominant trend so you can align your trades with the market's prevailing force. Each section builds naturally on the one before it.

Structural analysis is the cornerstone of the entire methodology. If this foundation is wrong, everything that follows becomes unreliable.

Basic Swing High/ Swing Low

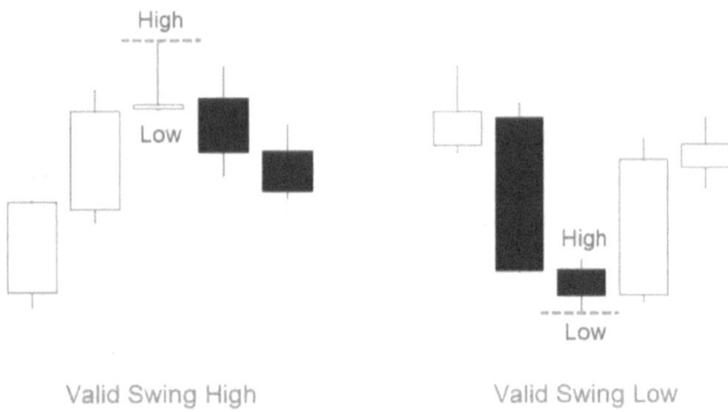

Figure 2.1: Swing High/ Swing Low

We begin with the most basic foundation: identifying a valid swing.

Figure 2.1 presents two examples—a valid swing high and a valid swing low. A swing is essentially a pivot point where price temporarily reverses before continuing in another direction. However, not every high or low you see on a chart qualifies as a meaningful swing. If you mark every minor fluctuation as a swing, your chart will quickly turn into an unreadable maze. A valid swing must meet clear and objective criteria.

The Five-Candle Rule for a Swing High

A valid swing high is identified through a sequence of five consecutive candles. The candle in the middle—the third candle in the sequence—acts as the pivot point and must satisfy two conditions at the same time.

The first condition (the high): The highest price (the high) of the pivot candle must be higher than the highs of the two candles on its left (candles 1 and 2) and also higher than the highs of the two candles on its right (candles 4 and 5). In other words, the pivot candle must have the highest high within the entire five-candle formation.

The second condition (the low): At the same time, the lowest price (the low) of the pivot candle must also be higher than the lows of the two candles on its left and higher than the lows of the two candles on its right.

Only when a five-candle sequence satisfies both of these conditions can we confirm a valid swing high. If either condition is violated—for example, if the pivot candle forms the highest high but its low is not higher than the surrounding candles—then the structure does not qualify and should be ignored.

The Five-Candle Rule for a Swing Low

A valid swing low follows the same logic as the swing high, but in reverse. It is also identified using a sequence of five consecutive candles, with the middle candle acting as the pivot. However, the conditions are flipped.

The first condition (the low): The lowest price (the low) of the pivot candle must be lower than the lows of the two candles on its left and lower than the lows of the two candles on its right. In other words, the pivot candle must have the lowest low within the entire five-candle formation.

The second condition (the high): At the same time, the highest price (the high) of the pivot candle must also be lower than the highs of the two candles on its left and lower than the highs of the two candles on its right.

When a five-candle formation satisfies both conditions, we can confirm a valid swing low.

Why Five Candles?

There is a clear reason why we use five candles rather than three or seven. Five candles provide enough context to confirm that price has genuinely pivoted at that point, rather than simply reacting to random noise or a brief moment of hesitation.

With two candles on each side of the pivot, you gain confirmation that momentum has shifted both before and after the turning point. If fewer candles are used—such as a three-candle pattern—you will end up identifying too many false swings, which quickly clutters the chart. On the other hand, requiring more candles—such as seven—can cause you to miss important pivots because the criteria become too strict.

Five candles represent a practical middle ground: a balance between sensitivity and reliability.

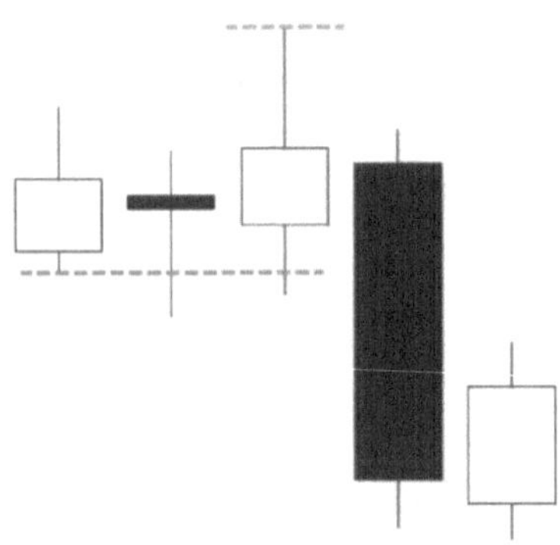

Figure 2.2: Invalid Swing High

As I emphasized earlier, not every high or low you see on a chart qualifies as a valid swing. Many candles may appear to be pivots at first glance, but they fail to meet the strict criteria. Let's examine a specific example in Figure 2.2 to make this clearer.

In Figure 2.2, we focus on the middle candle—the one that appears to be a potential swing high pivot. First, we check the first condition related to the high. The high of this candle is clearly higher than the highs of all four surrounding candles—two on the left and two on the right. So the requirement regarding the high is fully satisfied.

Now we move to the second condition concerning the low. This is where the structure fails. If we look carefully, the low of the pivot candle is not higher than the low of the first candle on the left. In fact, the pivot candle dips below that level. This violates the second condition, meaning the structure does not meet the full set of criteria.

As a result, even though the middle candle forms the highest high within the cluster, it does not qualify as a valid swing high under our strict five-candle rule. The conclusion is straightforward: this candle is simply part of normal price action—a minor high that does not carry enough significance to be marked as a structural pivot.

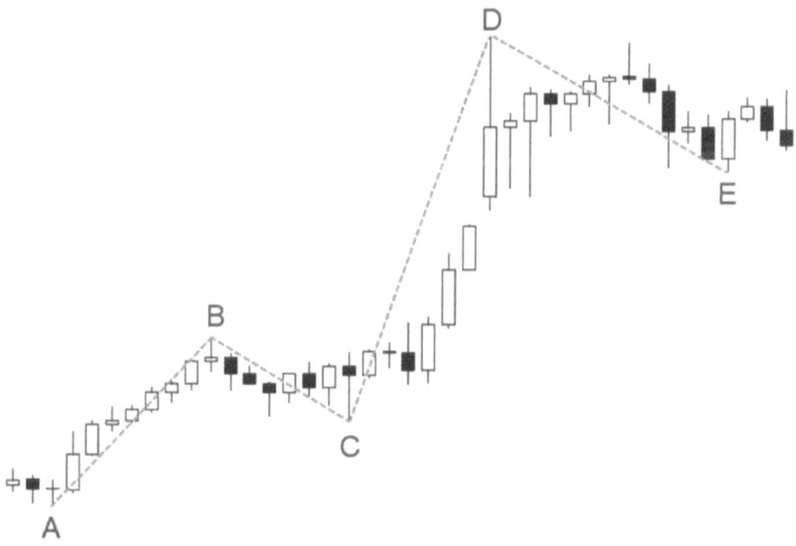

Figure 2.3: Chart Example

The purpose of identifying valid swings is not merely an academic exercise—it directly determines how you map the path of price and interpret market structure. This has a meaningful impact on your trading decisions. A small mistake in swing identification can easily cascade into a series of serious misinterpretations.

Let's look at Figure 2.3 to see the practical consequences of identifying swings incorrectly. In this chart, price moves from point A up to point B, then pulls back to point C, rallies strongly to point D, and finally declines toward point E.

Now suppose you make a mistake and mark point C as a valid swing low, even though it does not fully satisfy the five-candle rule. Specifically, at point **C**, the requirement related to the high is not met—the highs of the pivot candle are not lower than the highs of all the surrounding candles. But you overlook this detail and mark C as a swing low anyway.

What happens next? You end up drawing the price path as a zigzag pattern like the one shown in the chart: A → B → C → D → E, assuming that the market pivoted at B, C, and D.

However, because C is not a valid swing low according to our objective criteria, the structure you are analyzing is fundamentally incorrect. As a result, you may end up focusing on price zones that are not truly significant while overlooking areas that actually matter.

That is why identifying valid swings correctly is one of the most crucial steps in reading market structure.

Important Notes

Price patterns in financial markets come in many forms and are rarely perfect. In theory, the basic five-candle rule works smoothly: you identify the pivot candle, check the two candles on each side, verify the conditions, and the process is complete. In practice, however, price action does not always move in such a clean and orderly way. Markets often produce swing structures that are less obvious and more difficult to interpret, and traders need additional guidelines to handle these situations consistently.

Below are some advanced rules for identifying swings based on some of the most common structural variations in market behavior. These rules do not replace the basic five-candle rule; instead, they extend it to address situations that fall outside the typical pattern. By mastering these exceptions, you will be able to identify swings accurately across different market conditions—not just in ideal textbook examples.

Mother Candle – Inside Candle

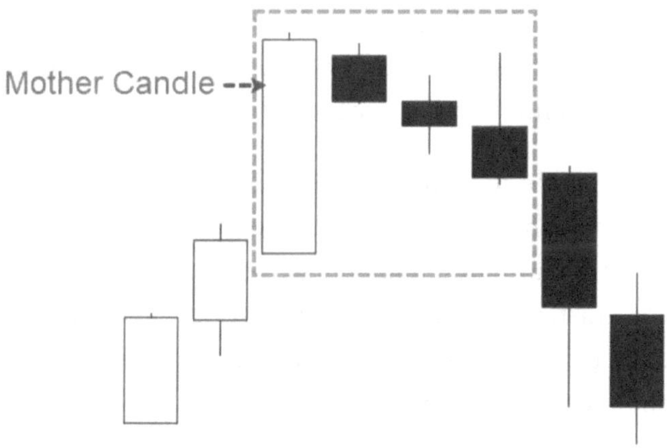

Figure 2.4: Mother candle

The first variation involves the **mother candle – inside candle** structure, illustrated in Figure 2.4. In this pattern, a candle with a very large range (the mother candle) completely engulfs several smaller candles that follow it (the inside candles).

In Figure 2.4, the highest price within the entire cluster is the high of the mother candle—the large candle whose range contains the three candles that come after it. If we apply the strict five-candle rule and treat this mother candle as the pivot within a standard five-candle formation, the structure would fail the criteria. The reason is that the low of the mother candle is not higher than the lows of all four surrounding candles. More specifically, the low of the mother candle is not higher than the lows of the inside candles on its right. Under a strict interpretation, this would mean that no valid swing high exists in this area.

However, this is a special case where an exception is allowed. When a mother–inside candle pattern appears, we can expand the evaluation unit and treat the entire group—the mother candle together with its inside candles—as a single cluster. Instead of counting each candle separately, we group them into one unit. The structure we evaluate is no longer five individual candles, but five elements: two candles on the left, the mother–inside cluster in the center, and two candles on the right.

Once the mother–inside formation is treated as a single unit, we compare the entire cluster with the surrounding candles. The high of this unit is the highest point within the whole cluster, while the low is the lowest point within that same cluster. Under this interpretation, the pattern satisfies the swing high criteria, and the highest point of the mother candle can be marked as a valid swing high pivot.

It is important to note, however, that expanding candle clusters does not always allow us to identify a valid swing high or swing low in every situation. Let's look at the example in Figure 2.5 to see why.

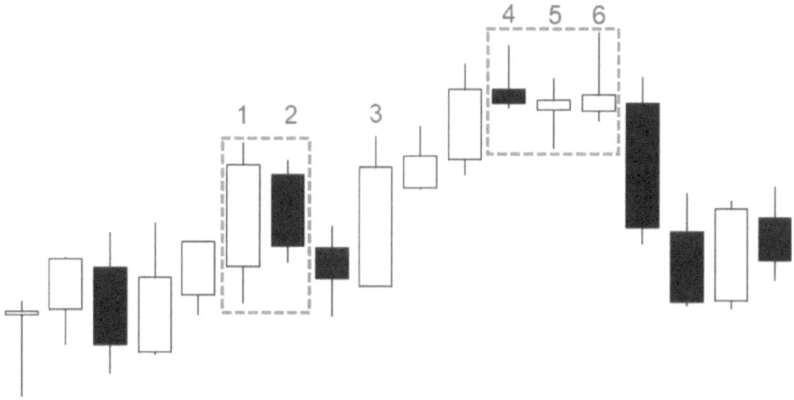

Figure 2.5: Valid & Invalid Swing Highs

In Figure 2.5, two clusters are highlighted: cluster 1–2 on the left and cluster 4–5–6 on the right.

Cluster 1–2 (Invalid): Let's start with candle 1 by itself. If we apply the basic five-candle rule, it does not qualify as a swing high because its low is not higher than the low of candle 2 on the right. Because of this, we might try expanding the structure and treating candles 1 and 2 as a mother–inside cluster. However, even after grouping them together, the structure still fails to meet the criteria.

Why? Because the high of the cluster is not higher than the high of candle 3, and the low of the cluster is not higher than the low of candle 3. In other words, the structure fails both conditions. As a result, no valid swing high exists within the region formed by candles 1 through 3. This is simply normal price movement, not a meaningful structural pivot.

Cluster 4–5–6 (Valid): Now let's examine the cluster on the right. If we evaluate candles 4, 5, or 6 individually, none of them satisfies the swing high criteria on its own. But when we combine all three candles into a single unit, the picture changes completely.

The cluster 4–5–6 is treated as one structure whose high is the highest point among the three candles and whose low is the lowest point among them. When we compare this cluster with the surrounding candles, both conditions are satisfied. The high of the cluster is higher than the highs of all four surrounding candles, and the low of the cluster is also higher than the lows of those same candles.

This means cluster 4–5–6 forms a valid swing high. The pivot point is marked at the highest point within the cluster—in this case, the high of candle 6.

Hopefully, this example helps you fully understand one of the most common variations you will encounter when identifying swing highs and swing lows in real market conditions.

Swing Highs and Swing Lows Depend on Each Other

A swing high should not be evaluated in isolation. It must always be considered in relation to the nearest swing low—and the same applies in the opposite direction. This is a critical principle that many traders often overlook.

Take a look at Figure 2.6 to understand why this dependency matters.

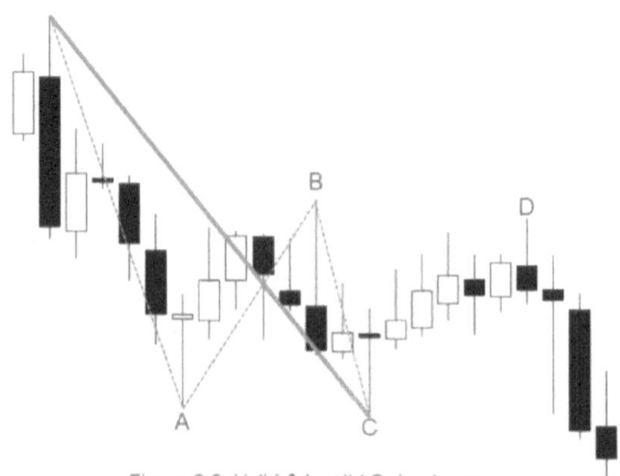

Figure 2.6: Valid & Invalid Swing Lows

Point A (Invalid Swing Low)

At first glance, point A appears to satisfy the criteria for a valid swing low. The high of A is lower than the highs of the four surrounding candles, and the low of A is lower than the lows of those same candles. If we evaluate it in isolation, both conditions seem to pass. However, the validation process does not stop there.

For A to truly qualify as a swing low, the subsequent swing high (point B) must also be valid. This is where the structure fails. When we examine point B, it does not satisfy the criteria for a swing high—no matter how the surrounding candles are grouped or expanded into clusters, B still fails the conditions.

This leads to a key insight: if the next swing high is not valid, the preceding swing low is automatically invalid as well. The reason is simple. Swing points only have meaning when they define a complete wave—from low to high or from high to low. If there is no valid high after A, there is no complete wave, and without a complete wave, A cannot be considered a structural pivot. In other words, the dashed zigzag line from A to B in the chart represents an incorrect interpretation of the structure.

Point C (Valid Swing Low)

Instead, point C is the valid swing low in this sequence. C not only satisfies the internal criteria—its highs and lows relative to the surrounding candles—but also passes the dependency test. The point that follows it, D, forms a fully valid swing high. Once D is confirmed as a valid swing high, C is automatically validated as a proper swing low.

This example highlights an important rule: when identifying swings, you cannot validate each point in isolation. You must evaluate the entire sequence. A swing low requires a subsequent valid swing high for confirmation, and a swing high requires a subsequent valid swing low to complete the structure.

Advanced Swing High/ Swing Low

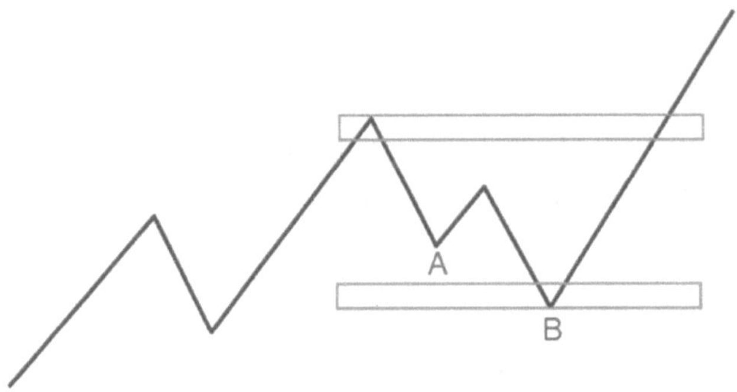

Figure 2.7: Swing High/ Swing Low

Now we move to the second part of the chapter—an upgrade to the analysis of swing identification. Part one taught you how to identify valid swings using the 5-candle rule. However, not every valid swing is equally important. This section will show you how to filter and evaluate swings within a broader context to identify the price levels that are truly critical for trading.

Take a look at the illustration in Figure 2.7. We have a clear uptrend structure. During the pullback, price forms two valid swing lows: point A and point B. Both satisfy the basic 5-candle rule. The question then becomes: which one is the confirmed swing low—the swing low that carries structural significance in this uptrend?

The answer is point B. This is the confirmed swing low because it satisfies two necessary conditions.

The first condition – the lowest point in the pullback structure:

Point B is the lowest point in the entire corrective wave. During a pullback in an uptrend, price may form multiple minor lows (such as point A), but only the lowest point of the entire correction qualifies as the structural swing low. Point A is not the lowest point—B is lower than A—so A does not qualify.

The second condition – the subsequent rally breaks the prior high:

After price touches point B, the next rally must break above the previous high (the high that existed before the pullback began). Point B satisfies this condition: the rally from B forms a higher high and clearly breaks above the prior high. This confirms that the uptrend has resumed after the correction.

In trading practice, your focus should be on the support at point B—the confirmed swing low—not at point A. If price later returns to retest the area, B is the critical level where you should watch for market reactions.

Figure 2.8: Swing lows

Figure 2.8 shows the application of this concept on a real chart. The chart presents an uptrend structure with two potential swing lows marked: point A and point B.

Analysis of point B (confirmed swing low):

Point B qualifies as a confirmed swing low because it satisfies both required conditions. The first condition is that B is the lowest point in the entire pullback structure. No other point in this corrective wave falls below B. The second condition is that the rally from B breaks above the prior high. The chart clearly shows that after touching B, price rallies strongly and breaks decisively above the previous high. This breakout confirms that the uptrend has resumed. Therefore, point B represents the structural swing low that traders should track.

Analysis of point A (intermediate swing only):

Point A fails to meet the conditions required for confirmation. The first issue is that A is not the lowest point in the pullback structure. Point B is significantly lower than A. The second issue is that the rally from A does not break the nearest prior swing high. The chart shows that the high formed after A remains below the previous high. This move represents only a temporary bounce within the correction rather than a true continuation of the uptrend. For this reason, point A is only an intermediate swing and does not carry structural significance.

This distinction has direct consequences for trading decisions. When a trader correctly identifies B as the structural swing low, the trader will wait for price to pull back toward the area around B and then look for long entry opportunities at that level. The logical target is the previous high or higher, and the stop loss is placed below B. This structure creates a clear and favorable risk–reward profile.

In contrast, an incorrect identification of A as the swing low leads to a flawed trading plan. A trader may attempt to enter long positions when price pulls back toward A. However, such an entry is premature because price can still decline further to B. Two different interpretations of swing lows therefore lead to two completely different trading approaches in terms of entry timing, stop placement, and risk–reward ratio.

Note: In an uptrend, traders should focus on identifying confirmed swing lows in order to locate key support levels. Swing highs only need to satisfy the basic 5-candle rule. In a downtrend, the logic is reversed: traders focus on confirmed swing highs to identify key resistance levels, while swing lows only require basic identification.

Valid Breakout

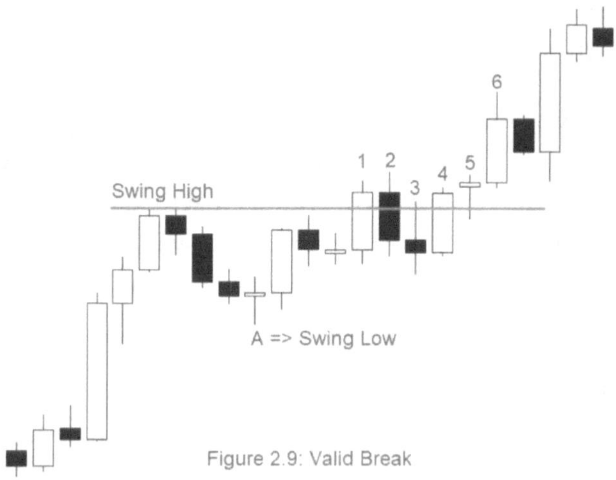

Figure 2.9: Valid Break

As mentioned earlier, a swing becomes a confirmed swing high or swing low only when price breaks the previous high or low. But what exactly qualifies as a valid break? This is a critical point that many traders misunderstand.

Breakout Principle

A break is confirmed only when a candle closes completely beyond the level of the previous swing. "Completely" means the entire candle—both the body and the wicks—must lie beyond the level. No part of the candle is allowed to touch or overlap the swing level. This is a strict rule, but it is necessary to avoid false breaks.

Figure 2.9 shows several candles testing a swing high level. Each candle provides an example of how the break criteria should be evaluated.

Candles 1, 2, 3, and 4 (failed breaks): All four candles fail to meet the break criteria. Although intraday price action briefly pushes above the swing high level and the wicks penetrate the level, most of each candle's body remains below it. This behavior shows that sellers still maintain control and push price back down before the close. Buyers do not demonstrate sufficient conviction. These candles represent attempted breaks, not confirmed breaks.

Candle 5 (nearly valid, but still invalid): Candle 5 appears much more convincing at first glance. Its body closes completely above the swing high level, which is a positive sign. However, a closer examination reveals that the lower wick still dips down and touches the swing high level. According to the strict definition, this candle still does not qualify as a valid break. It is very close, but it still fails the rule.

Candle 6 (valid break – confirmed): A truly valid break appears only at candle 6. The entire candle—both the body and the wicks (upper and lower)—lies completely above the swing high level. No part of the candle touches or overlaps the level. This candle represents a clean and decisive break. At this moment, buyers have clearly overcome the resistance level and pushed price fully beyond the previous stronghold of sellers. When candle 6 closes, point A officially becomes a confirmed swing low.

Why is this standard so strict? Breakouts are high-stakes moments in the market. If traders accept premature breaks—such as candles 4 or 5—they risk acting on false signals. The market can quickly reverse after such moves. A strict definition filters out noise and ensures that traders act only when real conviction is clearly demonstrated.

Identifying Structural Reversal Signals

Figure 2.10: Potential Trend Reversal

We now move to the next important part of the chapter—identifying when the market structure reverses. This skill is a key component of structural analysis because it identifies the moments when the trend changes direction.

Reversal from an Uptrend to a Downtrend

An uptrend structure reverses into a downtrend only when both of the following conditions are satisfied.

The first condition (necessary)

- Price must break below the most recent swing low.

The second condition (sufficient)

- After breaking the swing low, price must attempt a rally but fail to create a new high, forming a lower high during the retest.
- After that, price must decline again and create at least two lower lows relative to the swing low that was just broken.

Both conditions must occur for a valid structural reversal to be confirmed. If price breaks the swing low (the first condition) but then rallies strongly and breaks above the previous high instead of forming a lower high, the move represents a false break. In that situation, the market structure has not reversed, and the uptrend remains intact. This scenario represents one of the most common traps in trading, where traders call a reversal too early and enter against the prevailing trend before the structure has truly changed.

Reversal from a Downtrend to an Uptrend

The logic is the same as in the previous case, but in the opposite direction.

The first condition

- Price must break completely above the most recent swing high.

The second condition

- After the break occurs, the subsequent pullback must form a higher low.
- The rally that follows must create at least two higher highs relative to the swing high that was just broken.

Both conditions are mandatory. A break alone is not sufficient to confirm a structural reversal. The market must also demonstrate confirmation through the higher low–higher high pattern before the new uptrend structure can be considered valid.

2.11: Reversal of Structure

Figure 2.11 shows the application of the reversal criteria on a real chart. The chart presents the AUD/USD pair on the 1-hour timeframe. Horizontal lines are drawn through the swing high (SH) and swing low (SL) levels to clearly track the progression of the market structure.

Reversal analysis – the first condition is met: Starting from point 1, which represents the lowest point after the swing high is confirmed, price rallies toward the swing high resistance level. Several attempts occur, but the market is initially rejected, and price repeatedly fails to break the swing high. Only at candle 2 does price achieve a successful break above the swing high level, with the entire candle closing beyond the resistance. At this moment, the necessary condition for a reversal is satisfied because price produces a clean break above the swing high.

Awaiting the second condition: However, this step only satisfies the necessary condition and does not yet confirm a reversal. The market must now meet the sufficient condition. If price pulls back after candle 2, the subsequent movement must produce at least two higher highs relative to the swing high level. Only when a higher low–higher high sequence appears can we consider the possibility that an uptrend structure is forming. If price instead falls back and breaks below point 1 again, the move represents a false break, and the downtrend remains intact.

2.12: Failed Reversal of Structure

Figure 2.12 shows the actual price behavior after candle 2. This stage represents a critical test to determine whether the reversal is genuine.

After price breaks above the swing high and satisfies the necessary condition, the market does not continue rallying to form a higher high as required. Instead, price immediately turns and declines, forming a series of lower highs. The sufficient condition therefore fails to materialize. The chart does not show a higher low–higher high sequence, and the market does not confirm the formation of an uptrend structure.

As a result, the break at candle 2 represents only a temporary spike rather than a genuine structural reversal. The downtrend structure remains intact and continues to dominate the market.

In this situation, the correct bias remains bearish. Traders should continue looking for selling opportunities rather than chasing long positions. Many traders make a critical mistake at this point: they see the break above the swing high and immediately assume that a reversal has occurred. They switch their bias and begin buying, only to be caught in a false break and stopped out when the downtrend resumes.

Identifying the Dominant Trend

In the previous sections, we examined how to identify basic and advanced swing highs and swing lows, as well as the common variations that frequently appear in real market conditions. We also discussed how to determine valid breaks and how to recognize structural reversal signals. Together, these concepts provide the skills needed to identify the key levels that deserve attention in the market.

However, one final step remains: connecting all of this information to form a broader view of the market. In the final section of this chapter, we will examine a simple yet effective method for assessing the dominant trend of the market before moving on to the next stage of analysis—momentum.

Identifying a Downtrend

A market is considered to be in a downtrend when swing lows are repeatedly broken to the downside while swing highs remain unbroken to the upside. This pattern provides one of the clearest signs that selling pressure dominates the market.

Each time price attempts to recover and forms a swing high, it fails to break above the previous high. When the market turns downward again, price continues to break below prior swing lows and forms progressively lower lows. The repeated appearance of this pattern—failed rallies followed by new lows—is the defining characteristic of a strong downtrend.

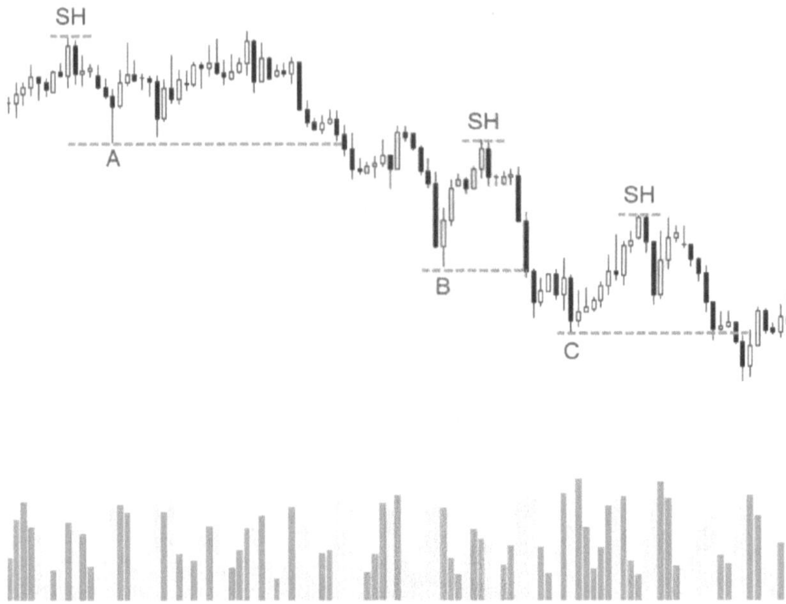

Figure 2.13: Downtrend

Figure 2.13 illustrates this pattern clearly. The market repeatedly forms new swing lows that break below the previous ones. Point B breaks below point A, point C then breaks below point B, and the sequence continues in the same manner. At the same time, each rally that forms a swing high fails to break above the previous swing high. This behavior defines a clear downtrend and creates an environment that is well suited for identifying short-selling opportunities.

Identifying an Uptrend

In contrast, a market is considered to be in an uptrend when swing highs are repeatedly broken to the upside while swing lows remain unbroken to the downside. This pattern indicates that buying pressure clearly dominates the market.

Each time price pulls back and forms a swing low, it fails to break below the previous low. When the market rallies again, price continues to break above prior swing highs and forms progressively higher highs. This structure represents the typical pattern of a strong uptrend, where each pullback is quickly absorbed and price continues its upward movement.

Figure 2.14: Uptrend

Figure 2.14 clearly illustrates this behavior. The market repeatedly breaks above previous swing highs—from point A to point B, then from point B to point C, and the sequence continues in the same manner. Each time price pulls back and forms a swing low, it respects the existing support levels and does not break below the previous swing low. This structure represents a typical uptrend and creates a favorable environment for identifying long entry opportunities.

Identifying a Sideways Market (Range-Bound Conditions)

When neither of the previous conditions is clearly present—when the market does not consistently break above swing highs and also does not consistently break below swing lows—the market is considered to be moving sideways. In this situation, price fluctuates within a defined range bounded by support on the lower side and resistance on the upper side.

Swing highs and swing lows tend to form around similar levels, creating a horizontal pattern rather than a diagonal progression. This structure reflects a temporary balance between buying and selling pressure, where neither side is strong enough to establish a clear directional trend.

Figure 2.15: Sideways market

Figure 2.15 illustrates this behavior clearly. Price repeatedly rebounds when it reaches the lower support area and is pushed back down when it approaches the upper resistance area. The swing highs occur at similar levels, forming a horizontal resistance line. Likewise, the swing lows appear at comparable levels, creating a horizontal support line.

In this situation, the market appears to be "trapped" within a box. There is no sustained upward trend and no sustained downward trend—price simply oscillates back and forth within the range. This type of environment is often the most difficult to trade, and traders should generally avoid it or wait for a clear breakout before taking new positions.

The Importance of Trading with the Trend

Our goal in trading is to operate in a trending market. The reason is simple: in a clear uptrend, the probability of successful long positions is significantly higher because you are trading in the same direction as the dominant flow of capital. Similarly, in a clear downtrend, short positions tend to have a higher success rate. In contrast, a sideways market makes both directions difficult to trade because there is no clear trend to follow.

Once you identify the dominant trend using this simple method—observing which swings are consistently being broken—you already gain a significant advantage. The next step is to search for high-quality entry points based on momentum, which is exactly what we will explore in the upcoming chapters.

At this point, you have completed the essential foundation layer of momentum trading. The 5-candle rule provides an objective method for identifying valid swings. Confirmed swings help you mark key support and resistance levels. The reversal criteria prevent premature bias shifts. The trend-assessment framework gives you immediate context for every trading decision.

This structural mastery is a prerequisite that cannot be skipped. With the skills from this chapter, you gain the ability to read the "map" of the market—you understand where price currently stands, the direction it is moving, and the moments when the structure may potentially shift. However, structure alone only tells you *where* the market is and *where it might go*. It does not answer the critical question: Is the move strong enough?

That question is addressed by momentum—the second M in the SMT framework. In the next chapters, we will study momentum in depth, beginning with the concept of volume in trading, where I will show you the evidence that demonstrates its reliability.

CHAPTER 3: UNDERSTANDING VOLUME

The first two chapters have provided you with the foundation of market structure. You have learned how to identify basic and advanced swing points, determine the dominant trend, and recognize potential reversals. However, as you saw in Chapter 1, two trends can share a very similar structure yet display completely different levels of strength. One trend advances rapidly with clear conviction, while another moves slowly and hesitantly, lacking decisiveness. That difference is momentum.

Momentum measures the strength of price movements. It answers a critical question: *Does this trend have genuine strength?* Strong momentum confirms that a trend is likely to continue, while weak momentum warns of a potential reversal. This chapter is the first of several that will explore this concept in depth.

The Role of Volume

Momentum analysis is closely tied to volume. Volume reveals truths that price alone can sometimes conceal. Price may rally while volume remains low—suggesting false strength. Price may decline with rising volume—indicating genuine distribution. In this sense, volume represents proof of conviction. However, before diving into volume analysis, we must address an important question: tick volume versus real volume—are they different, and does the difference matter? What does the evidence say?

Many traders question the value of volume in trading. They argue that volume is only reliable in centralized markets such as stocks, where all transactions are fully reported. In decentralized markets like Forex or cryptocurrencies, volume does not reflect the total activity of the entire market. Each exchange reports only its own volume. The data is fragmented and incomplete. Based on this reasoning, some conclude that volume in these markets is meaningless and should be ignored altogether.

In trading, however, volume does not need to be perfect to be useful. What matters is not the absolute accuracy of the volume figures, but the relative patterns that volume reveals. This chapter will clarify the nature of volume across different types of markets and present empirical evidence on the correlation between tick volume and real volume. Most importantly, it will provide a systematic framework for applying volume analysis correctly.

Volume in Different Markets

Before we go further, it is important to distinguish the nature of volume across the three major types of markets. Each has its own characteristics, which directly influence how we should interpret volume data.

The stock market provides the ideal environment for volume analysis. It is a centralized market—every transaction is executed through a single exchange such as New York Stock Exchange, NASDAQ, or London Stock Exchange. This centralization means that the volume displayed on the chart reflects the full trading activity of the market. Every share bought and every contract sold is captured and reported by the exchange. As a result, the volume data you see represents the actual volume traded. Each volume figure corresponds directly to real transactions that have taken place in the market. In its purest definition, this is real volume—a direct measurement of supply and demand interacting through actual trades.

The situation is fundamentally different in **Forex** and **cryptocurrency** markets. Both operate in a decentralized environment. Trading takes place simultaneously across many different venues rather than through a single centralized exchange. In the Forex market, trading occurs within the interbank network, where banks, brokers, and institutional participants trade directly with one another through private systems. In the cryptocurrency market, trading activity is spread across numerous exchanges such as Binance, Coinbase, and Bybit, each reporting its own separate volume data. This decentralized structure creates a fundamental challenge: it is impossible to aggregate the true total trading volume of the entire market.

For this reason, the volume displayed on retail trading platforms such as MetaTrader 4, MetaTrader 5, or TradingView is not real volume. Instead, it represents tick volume, which is a different type of measurement. Tick volume does not measure the number of contracts or units traded. Rather, it measures how many times price changes—how many price ticks occur—within a given period of time. Each time price moves from one level to another, it is counted as a tick. Whether that movement is caused by a single lot or by a thousand lots, it is still recorded as one tick.

For example, consider a 5-minute candle in the EUR/USD market. Suppose price moves from 1.0850 to 1.0870 during that period. If the price action is choppy, with many small fluctuations—1.0851, 1.0852, 1.0853, 1.0854, and so on—tick volume will be very high because the platform records hundreds of individual price changes. By contrast, if price moves from 1.0850 to 1.0870 in a relatively straight line with only a few intermediate ticks, the recorded volume will be much lower, even though the overall magnitude of the move is exactly the same.

The logic behind the tick-volume methodology is quite reasonable. When market activity is intense—when many participants are placing orders and many transactions are being executed—price tends to fluctuate rapidly. Rapid fluctuations generate more ticks. As a result, high tick volume generally suggests high trading activity, while low tick volume indicates lower activity.

The Truth About Tick Volume

The key question, however, is whether this assumption is supported by real data. Is the correlation between tick volume and real volume strong enough for traders to rely on it with confidence?

Fortunately, we do not have to rely on speculation—empirical research has already addressed this question. A study by Caspar Marney (2011) conducted a comprehensive analysis comparing tick volume with actual traded volume from two of the world's largest ECNs: Hotspot FX and EBS. These sources provide institutional-grade data that captures a significant portion of global FX transactions rather than retail-level estimates.

The research examined four major currency pairs—EUR/USD, USD/JPY, GBP/USD, and EUR/CHF—across multiple months in order to ensure consistency and reduce the impact of anomalies.

The results were remarkably clear. The Pearson correlation coefficient between tick volume and real traded volume ranged from 0.9583 to 0.9894, depending on the currency pair. To put these numbers into perspective, a correlation of 1.0 represents perfect correlation, while 0.0 indicates no correlation at all. In financial research, any correlation above 0.95 is considered exceptionally strong.

More specifically, EUR/USD showed a correlation of 0.9683, meaning that about 96.8% of the variation in tick volume could be explained by movements in actual traded volume. GBP/USD showed an even higher correlation of 0.9894, implying that 98.9% of the variation in tick volume directly reflected changes in real trading activity.

Even more important than the statistical correlation is the visual pattern matching observed in the study. The research overlaid charts of real volume and tick volume across different hours of the trading day. The results were striking. When real volume spiked during peak trading periods—particularly the London–New York session overlap—tick volume spiked at exactly the same times with nearly identical magnitude. When real volume declined during the quieter Asian session, tick volume mirrored that decline almost perfectly.

In other words, the overall shape of the volume profile—its peaks, troughs, gradual rises, and sudden drops—remained highly synchronized between tick volume and real volume. The only meaningful difference lay in the absolute numbers, not in the behavioral patterns they revealed.

The study concludes explicitly: *"From a statistical standpoint, participants in the foreign exchange markets should feel safe to use tick volume as a proxy for actual traded volume."* This statement is not merely an opinion—it is a conclusion drawn from rigorous quantitative analysis of real institutional trading data.

The implication is clear. Tick volume is not a perfect substitute for real volume, but it is a highly reliable proxy for the purposes of pattern recognition and momentum analysis. In other words, while tick volume does not measure the exact number of contracts traded, it still reflects the underlying dynamics of market participation with remarkable accuracy.

The bottom line is straightforward: tick volume works. You can trust the volume patterns you observe on platforms such as MetaTrader 4, MetaTrader 5, or TradingView. When you see a spike in volume, it reflects a genuine increase in market activity. When volume begins to dry up, it signals a real decline in participation.

The absolute numbers themselves are not what matter most. What truly matters are the relative patterns revealed by the data. And those patterns in tick volume mirror the behavior of real trading volume with a correlation exceeding 95%, which is more than sufficient for practical trading analysis.

You can download the full study here: https://shorturl.at/Xgda4

Figure 3.1: Tick Volume Across Different Brokers

Another concern traders often raise is this: if each broker provides slightly different data, can volume analysis still be consistent? This is a reasonable concern. In practice, however, data from major brokers tends to be highly synchronized. For example, when comparing EUR/USD tick volume on the H1 timeframe between OANDA and FXCM, the correlation exceeds 90%.

More specifically, sudden spikes in volume, periods of gradually declining activity, and the timing of major peaks tend to align closely across both brokers. The main difference lies only in the absolute magnitude. One broker might show a peak of around 19,000 ticks, while another might display 25,000 ticks. Despite this numerical difference, the relative pattern remains essentially identical. As a result, a trader using OANDA and a trader using FXCM will typically arrive at the same conclusion regarding the strength or weakness of a trend—the only difference lies in the raw numbers displayed.

Empirical evidence consistently confirms that tick volume is a reliable proxy for real trading volume. A correlation close to 90% is not perfect, but it is strong enough to support sound trading decisions. No analytical tool in trading offers 100% accuracy, and rejecting volume analysis simply because it is not "perfect" would be similar to rejecting price action analysis because it occasionally produces false signals.

The key point is this: if you understand how to read volume correctly, the difference between tick volume and real volume does not significantly reduce its analytical value. Traders need a tool that helps them measure market participation and conviction, and tick volume provides exactly that.

However, understanding the nature of volume is only the first step. Using it effectively requires a clear analytical framework. The following sections introduce the fundamental principles for analyzing momentum through volume.

Principles for Trading with Volume

First principle: Structure first, volume second. Never reverse this order

Structure defines the context—whether the market is in an uptrend, a downtrend, or a sideways range. Volume then reveals the strength or weakness of that context. When you analyze structure first, you understand the direction in which the market is moving. Volume analysis then tells you whether that movement carries genuine conviction.

For example, imagine a market that is clearly trending upward, forming a series of higher highs and higher lows. This is a bullish structure. However, if volume gradually declines with each rally, the bullish structure is losing strength and may be approaching exhaustion. By contrast, if you notice a single candle with a sudden surge in volume but do not understand the structural context, you cannot determine whether that activity represents buying exhaustion or strong buying continuation. For this reason, the sequence of analysis must never be reversed.

Second principle: Prioritize volume trends rather than isolated volume spikes

Volume trends are patterns in which volume gradually increases or decreases across multiple waves of price movement. For example, consider a downtrend in which volume expands with each successive decline: the first downward swing shows volume X, the second decline shows higher volume, and the third decline shows even higher participation. This pattern suggests that each wave of selling involves greater participation than the previous one. Sellers are increasing their conviction, and the downtrend is strengthening.

The opposite pattern also provides valuable information. Suppose an uptrend develops in which the first rally occurs with high volume, the second rally with lower volume, and the third rally with even weaker volume. In this situation, buyers are gradually losing interest, and the uptrend is becoming fragile. Progressive patterns like these are usually clearer and more reliable because they reveal the evolving behavior of market participants.

By contrast, an isolated volume spike—such as a single candle showing unusually high volume within a sideways range—is far more difficult to interpret. Without sufficient context, a single spike can be ambiguous. For that reason, it is generally more effective to focus first on gradual volume patterns before attempting to interpret individual spikes.

Third principle: Analyze individual candlesticks only when price approaches key zones

Most of the time, volume should be evaluated at the level of price waves—by observing the overall volume associated with an entire upward swing or downward swing. However, when price approaches critical areas—such as major support or resistance levels, previous highs or lows, or psychologically significant round numbers—it becomes necessary to zoom in and examine the volume of individual candlesticks.

At these locations, traders look for divergences between price action and volume behavior. For example, price may test a resistance level with a large bullish candle that appears strong on the surface. Yet if that candle forms on unusually low volume, the underlying participation is weak. Price action appears convincing, but volume reveals a lack of commitment behind the move. Situations like this often signal a potential rejection rather than a genuine breakout.

We will examine these candle-level techniques in greater detail in the later sections of this book.

Fourth principle (specific to Forex): Normalize volume across trading sessions

The first three principles apply to all financial markets. However, the Forex market has a unique structural characteristic: session-based volume disparity. Although Forex operates 24 hours a day, liquidity is not evenly distributed throughout the day. The market transitions through three major trading sessions—the Asian session (Tokyo), the European session (London), and the U.S. session (New York)—and each of these sessions exhibits very different volume characteristics.

The U.S. session typically shows significantly higher trading activity than the Asian session. The European session often records the highest volume overall, especially during the period when London overlaps with New York. By contrast, the Asian session usually displays the lowest participation.

This disparity creates a fundamental analytical problem: comparing volume across different sessions is essentially comparing apples to oranges. A candle that represents "normal volume" during the New York session may easily exceed what would be considered "high volume" during the Tokyo session. The baseline level of activity is completely different. If you compare volume across sessions without adjusting for this difference, your conclusions can easily become misleading.

To analyze volume accurately, traders generally use one of two approaches.

First approach: use higher timeframes such as D1, W1, or MN. At these timeframes, each candle incorporates all trading sessions within a 24-hour period. Volume therefore becomes automatically normalized. A high-volume day reflects elevated activity across the combined sessions, which eliminates the problem of session-based disparities.

Second approach: when trading intraday, compare volume only within the same session. For example, if you trade the U.S. session, compare the volume of candles formed at 10:00 AM EST with those at 11:00 AM EST or 2:00 PM EST—times that all belong to the same New York trading window. In this case, the comparison remains valid because the baseline level of participation is consistent. What you should avoid is comparing candles from the U.S. session with candles from the Asian session.

As a practical illustration, a volume spike observed at 10:00 AM EST should be compared with the average volume of other U.S. session hours (approximately 9:30 AM–4:00 PM EST), rather than with the 24-hour average that includes the typically quiet Asian hours.

Fifth principle: Choose a reliable data source

As discussed earlier, major brokers tend to show high correlation with one another and with institutional data sources. However, smaller brokers or poorly regulated platforms may provide inaccurate—or even manipulated—data. Since data quality directly affects analytical quality, unreliable data will inevitably lead to unreliable conclusions.

In the Forex market, it is generally best to rely on large, well-regulated brokers. FXCM and OANDA are two commonly cited examples whose tick-volume data has been validated in independent research. Both firms have long operational histories and operate under strict regulatory oversight, making their data suitable for volume analysis.

In the cryptocurrency market, traders should prioritize major exchanges such as Binance, Coinbase, or Bybit. These platforms maintain deep liquidity and generally report genuine trading activity. Smaller exchanges should be approached with caution, as wash trading—artificially inflated volume designed to attract traders—is relatively common in such environments. In markets like crypto, real liquidity matters.

Together, these five principles form the foundation for all volume analysis you will perform. They are not rigid rules but practical guidelines designed to help you interpret volume correctly and avoid common analytical traps. The first principle ensures that your analysis always begins with structural context. The second directs your attention toward meaningful patterns rather than random noise. The third focuses your analysis on the most critical price zones. The fourth addresses the unique challenges of the Forex market. The fifth ensures that your analysis is built on reliable data.

In the next chapter, we will expand our understanding of market dynamics by exploring three fundamental laws developed by Richard Wyckoff—one of the most influential figures in the history of technical analysis. We will also introduce Volume Spread Analysis (VSA), a powerful framework that many traders consider a true game changer in momentum trading.

CHAPTER 4: THE THREE LAWS OF VOLUME ANALYSIS

This chapter focuses on three fundamental laws of volume analysis: the Law of Supply and Demand, the Law of Cause and Effect, and the Law of Effort versus Result. These three principles are not only the foundation of the methodology presented in this book, but also core concepts that will appear repeatedly throughout the chapters that follow. More importantly, they provide a conceptual framework that you can expand and apply throughout your entire trading career—not only within the scope of momentum trading.

These three laws deserve careful study. They are not mechanical rules to be applied rigidly, but rather lenses through which you can observe market behavior at a deeper level. Each law reveals a different aspect of the relationship between price and volume. Taken together, they form a coherent picture of how markets actually move.

In the sections that follow, I will explain each law with concrete examples and practical applications. The goal is not only to help you understand the concepts, but also to show you how to apply them in real trading situations—particularly when analyzing momentum.

Spread

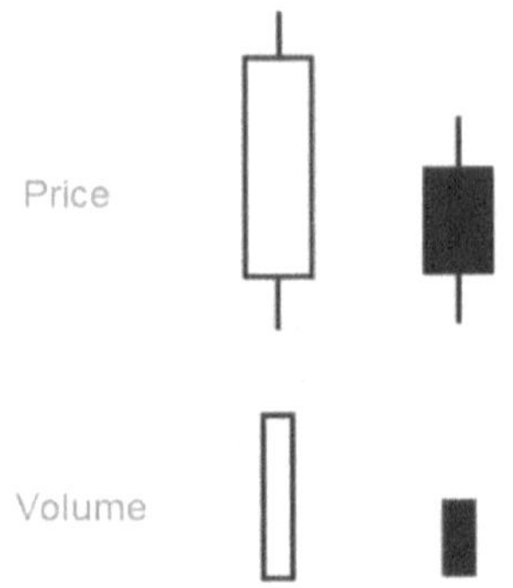

Figure 4.1: Price and Volume

Before we examine the three laws, let's first establish a fundamental concept: spread.

Spread is the distance between the high and the low of a candlestick. A candle with a wide spread indicates strong price movement—the market traveled a significant distance during that timeframe. A candle with a narrow spread indicates weak price movement—price fluctuated only within a tight range. In other words, spread reflects the magnitude of price change.

Spread, when analyzed together with volume, forms the basis of Volume Spread Analysis (VSA)—one of the most important components in momentum analysis.

Consider Figure 4.1. Two candles are presented: a white candle on the left and a black candle on the right. The white candle has a wide spread (a large body and broad range) accompanied by high volume (a tall volume bar). The black candle, by contrast, has a narrow spread (a small body and tight range) with low volume (a small volume bar).

The interpretation is straightforward. The white candle reflects strong buying participation—many buyers are active, pushing price upward and producing a large upward movement. The black candle reflects a weak selling attempt—few sellers are participating, price barely moves, and the result is a small downward move. In this comparison, buyers clearly dominate.

Why is this relationship so important? Because in real trading, you will constantly encounter situations where spread and volume do not align so neatly as they do in Figure 4.1. For example, you may see a candle with a wide spread but low volume—meaning price travels far despite limited participation. Or you may observe a candle with a narrow spread but unusually high volume—indicating intense activity but very little net price movement.

These mismatches between spread and volume often carry important meaning. In many cases, they signal potential turning points, hidden accumulation or distribution, or even market traps. As we progress through this chapter, you will learn how to recognize these different spread–volume relationships and decode the implications they carry for real trading decisions.

The Law of Supply and Demand

The first law we examine in this chapter forms the foundation of all market mechanics: the Law of Supply and Demand.

This law states a simple yet powerful principle: price rises when demand exceeds supply, and price falls when supply exceeds demand. It is a fundamental economic principle and also a core concept in the analytical framework developed by Richard Wyckoff for understanding market behavior.

In any market, three possible states can occur:

Supply > Demand: Sellers overwhelm buyers → price declines. The market is in an imbalance tilted toward sellers.

Demand > Supply: Buyers overwhelm sellers → price rises. The market is in an imbalance tilted toward buyers.

Supply = Demand: The forces are balanced → price moves sideways with no clear direction. The market is in a state of equilibrium.

Every price movement you observe on a chart is the result of one of these three states. Understanding this principle is the starting point for decoding market behavior through volume analysis.

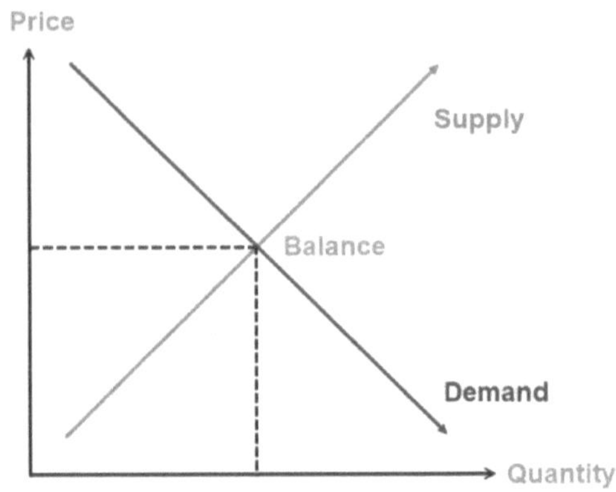

Figure 4.2: The Law of Supply and Demand

Figure 4.2 illustrates the classic supply–demand model from economics. The horizontal axis (Quantity) represents trading volume, while the vertical axis (Price) represents the price level. The two curves intersect at the equilibrium point—labeled **Balance** and marked by a dashed line.

The **supply curve** slopes upward from left to right. The logic behind this relationship is straightforward: as prices rise, sellers become increasingly willing to provide more supply to the market. Higher prices translate into more attractive profit margins, which naturally incentivize additional selling. In other words, the higher the price climbs, the more market participants are motivated to sell.

The **demand curve**, by contrast, slopes downward from left to right. When prices rise, buyers tend to reduce their willingness to purchase because the asset becomes more expensive. Conversely, when prices fall, buyers become more eager to enter the market because the asset appears more affordable. Lower prices therefore stimulate demand, encouraging buyers to accumulate larger quantities.

The **equilibrium point**, labeled **Balance**, is where the two curves intersect. At this point, the quantity supplied equals the quantity demanded. There is neither a shortage nor a surplus in the market. Supply is precisely sufficient to satisfy demand, and both buyers and sellers are comfortable transacting at that particular price level.

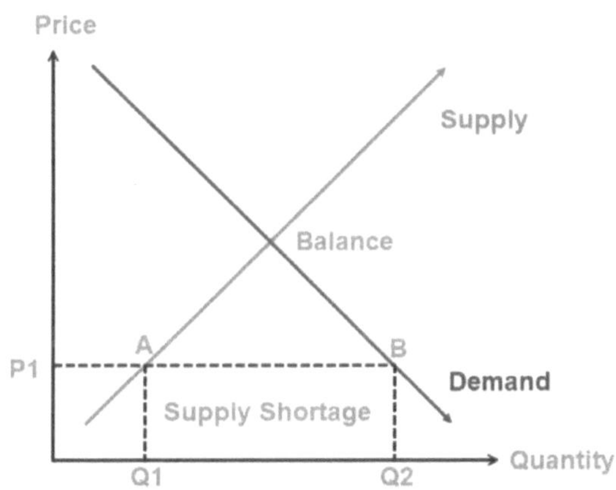

Figure 4.3: The Law of Supply and Demand

Figure 4.3 illustrates a situation of **supply shortage**. At the price level $\mathbf{P_1}$—which lies below the equilibrium—a critical imbalance appears in the market.

At the price level $\mathbf{P_1}$, sellers are willing to supply only quantity $\mathbf{Q_1}$ (point A on the supply curve). The reason is simple: the price is too low to motivate greater participation from sellers, so there is little incentive for them to provide more supply. At the same time, buyers view this price as attractive. As a result, they are willing to demand a much larger quantity,

$\mathbf{Q_2}$ (point B on the demand curve). The gap between $\mathbf{Q_2}$ and $\mathbf{Q_1}$ represents a **supply shortage**—demand significantly exceeds the available supply.

The inevitable consequence of this imbalance is upward pressure on price. Because many buyers are competing for a limited amount of supply, the competition among them intensifies. Some buyers begin offering higher prices in order to secure trades, while sellers recognize their advantage and start raising their asking prices. In some cases, higher prices may also encourage additional sellers to enter the market and increase supply. Either way, the imbalance pushes the market upward toward equilibrium.

This process illustrates the mechanics of a **bullish imbalance**: when demand exceeds supply, price rises.

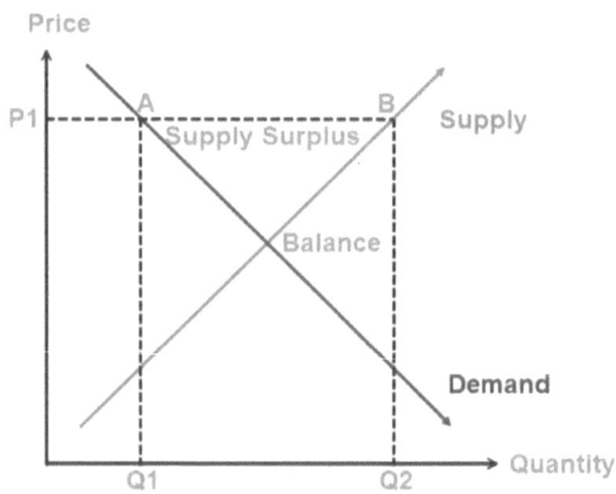

Figure 4.4: The Law of Supply and Demand

Figure 4.4 illustrates the opposite situation—a **supply surplus**. At the price level $\mathbf{P_1}$, which lies above the equilibrium, a different imbalance emerges, but this time in the opposite direction.

At this higher price level $\mathbf{P_1}$, sellers are willing to supply quantity $\mathbf{Q_1}$ (point A on the supply curve) because the price is attractive for selling. Higher prices naturally encourage sellers to bring more supply into the market. However, at the same price level, buyers are willing to demand only quantity $\mathbf{Q_2}$ (point B on the demand curve). The price is simply too high to be appealing, so fewer buyers are prepared to participate. The gap between **Q_1** and **Q_2** represents a **supply surplus**—the available supply significantly exceeds the level of demand.

The inevitable consequence of this imbalance is downward pressure on price. Sellers begin competing with one another to find buyers for their excess inventory. In order to attract demand, they must lower their asking prices, or reduce the amount of supply offered until it reaches a level that buyers are willing to absorb. This competitive pressure gradually drives the price back down toward equilibrium.

This process illustrates the mechanics of a bearish imbalance: when supply exceeds demand, price declines.

In practical chart analysis, traders evaluate supply–demand imbalances by observing three key elements: the closing price, the spread, and the volume. For example, a bullish candle with a wide spread, a close near its high, and high volume typically signals that demand is overwhelming supply. Buyers are aggressive, pushing the market strongly upward. Conversely, a bearish candle with a wide spread, a close near its low, and high volume indicates that supply is overwhelming demand. Sellers dominate the order flow and drive price sharply lower.

Recognizing these patterns allows traders to identify supply–demand imbalances directly on the chart, often in real time.

The Law of Cause and Effect

We now move to the second law—the Law of Cause and Effect. This principle appears everywhere in life and follows a simple logic: every result has a cause behind it. For example, if we have apples to eat (the effect), it is because someone previously planted apple trees (the cause). In a trading context, this principle translates into the following idea: when price makes a strong rally or a sharp decline (the effect), it is usually preceded by a preparation phase during which positions are built up (the cause).

Accumulation and Distribution - Two Important Phases

Before explaining the law further, you need to understand these two concepts. Accumulation is the phase in which smart money quietly buys and absorbs supply during a sideways consolidation, preparing for a potential upward move. Distribution is the phase in which smart money quietly sells and offloads positions to buyers during a sideways consolidation, preparing for a potential downward move. These two phases represent the cause that later produces trending moves in the market.

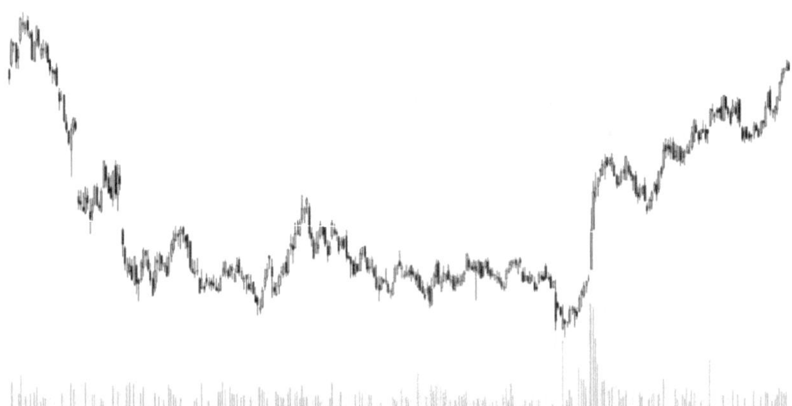

Figure 4.5: The Law of Cause and Effect

Figure 4.5 demonstrates this law clearly. The strong rally on the right side of the chart occurs after a prolonged accumulation phase on the left. During this phase, smart money systematically absorbs supply from floating sellers in the market in a patient and methodical manner. Once enough supply has been absorbed and willing sellers are largely exhausted, price can rally easily because there is no longer significant resistance above to block the momentum.

The key insight is that the longer the accumulation phase lasts, the stronger and more sustained the subsequent rally tends to be—**a larger cause produces a larger effect**.

Figure 4.6: The Law of Cause and Effect

Figure 4.6 illustrates a similar relationship for downside movements. The sharp decline highlighted on the chart occurs after a prolonged distribution phase within the sideways range above. During this phase, smart money gradually and systematically distributes their positions to eager buyers below. They continue offloading supply until there is no longer sufficient demand to absorb it. At that point, price declines sharply because buyers' support has largely disappeared.

After the decline, price enters a short consolidation phase where some accumulation takes place, producing a brief rally. However, this rally is weak and short-lived because the accumulation phase was too brief—an insufficient cause produces only a weak effect. Price then enters another distribution phase and continues declining.

The Law of Effort and Result

We now move to the final law—and the one with the most practical application among the three principles presented in this chapter—the **Law**

of Effort and Result, a concept that will become a core component of your momentum analysis.

This law states that price action should be reflected by volume levels in a proportional way. Volume represents effort—the amount of energy and participation invested in the market by all participants. Spread, or price movement, represents the result—the visible outcome of that effort on the chart. The fundamental logic is straightforward: a large effort, reflected in high volume, should produce a large result, reflected in a wide spread. Conversely, a small effort, reflected in low volume, should produce a small result, reflected in a narrow spread.

When this relationship remains in harmony—high volume accompanied by wide spreads, or low volume accompanied by narrow spreads—market behavior is normal and consistent with natural market dynamics. Price movements align logically with the level of participation behind them. In such situations, there are no unusual anomalies to be concerned about, and the prevailing trend can often continue smoothly in its current direction.

However, when effort and result fail to match proportionally, anomalies begin to appear. These divergences often provide extremely powerful trading signals that traders must learn to recognize. Consider the illustration in Figure 4.7 below.

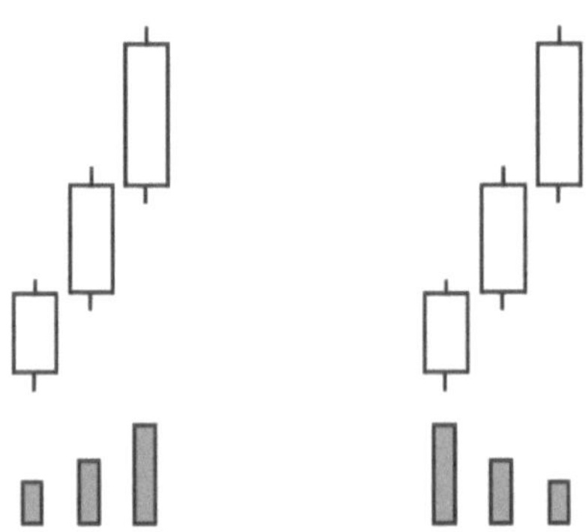

Figure 4.7: Confirmation and Divergence

Figure 4.7 illustrates two contrasting scenarios of the law of effort and result. The chart on the left shows confirmation—a healthy uptrend where rising prices are accompanied by steadily increasing volume. This pattern indicates a sustainable uptrend because the price increase is supported by growing participation from new buyers entering the market, suggesting that demand is strengthening. In this case, there is clear harmony between effort (rising volume) and result (rising prices), allowing us to expect that the upward trend is likely to continue.

The chart on the right shows divergence, which serves as a critical warning signal. Price continues to rise, but volume gradually declines, creating a mismatch between result and effort. Declining volume means fewer buyers are willing to chase higher prices, participation is shrinking, and the uptrend is progressively losing strength. This lack of volume support suggests that the move may become vulnerable to a reversal once selling pressure appears.

Now let us move to Figure 4.8 below to better understand another example of imbalance between price and volume.

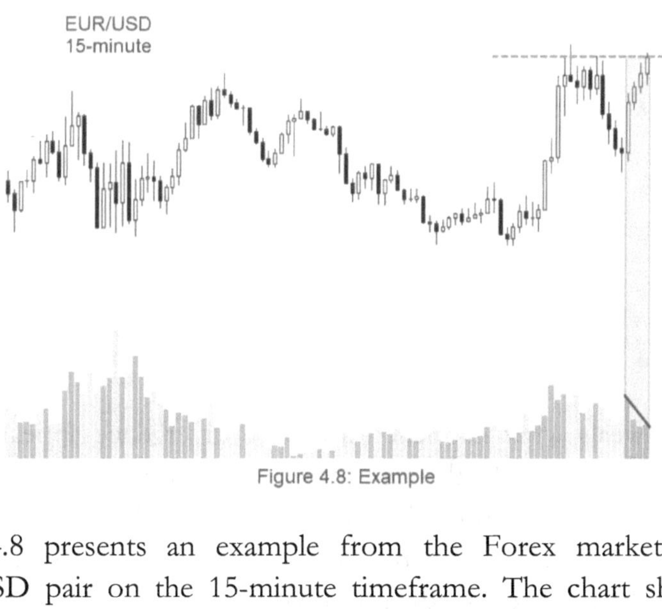

Figure 4.8: Example

Figure 4.8 presents an example from the Forex market using the EUR/USD pair on the 15-minute timeframe. The chart shows a key resistance zone marked above. As price rallies toward this resistance, we can see a sequence of bullish candles forming. However, the effort behind this move is missing, because volume steadily declines throughout the rally, as indicated in the volume panel.

This is a classic divergence—price rises while volume falls, indicating that the result is not supported by the corresponding effort. Such a pattern reveals that the rally lacks conviction, is unlikely to be sustainable, and has a high probability of reversal. When price approaches resistance with this type of volume behavior, it should be treated as a warning signal. If you are holding long positions, it may be wise to consider taking profits, as price is likely to face rejection at resistance and move lower.

Let us see what happens next in the following figure.

Figure 4.9: Example

Figure 4.9 reveals what happened after the divergence appeared. Price quickly declined and broke through the previous swing low, establishing a clear downtrend. This move is the direct consequence of the earlier mismatch between effort and result—the warning signal of a potential reversal that the law had already indicated.

Analyzing Volume Relationships Between Waves

Now we move to the final section of this chapter—learning how to anticipate potential changes in market structure by observing volume patterns across waves. Waves provide valuable data about shifts taking place in the balance between supply and demand. By comparing volume across waves, we can project with a reasonable degree of confidence whether a trend is likely to continue or reverse. Two fundamental approaches can be used: comparing volume between waves moving in the same direction (impulse waves), and comparing volume between waves moving in opposite directions (impulse versus corrective waves).

Let us begin with the first approach.

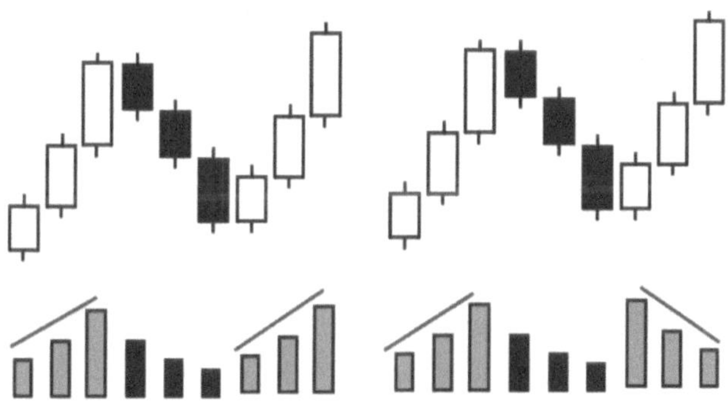

Figure 4.10: Price - Volume Correlation

Figure 4.10 illustrates two scenarios showing how volume behavior across consecutive impulse waves can reveal the health of a trend. The illustration on the left demonstrates a case of sustained trend strength. The first upward wave shows clear volume progression, with volume increasing throughout the wave, indicating strong participation. The second upward wave displays the same pattern, with volume continuing to expand. This behavior confirms that the uptrend still maintains strong conviction and has a high probability of continuing, because each new impulse wave attracts a level of participation comparable to—or even greater than—the previous one, indicating that demand remains robust.

The illustration on the right presents the opposite scenario, which serves as a warning sign of a weakening trend. The first upward wave shows a healthy volume progression, with volume increasing throughout the move. However, the second upward wave exhibits a declining volume pattern, where volume decreases rather than increases. This divergence between successive impulse waves reveals that the uptrend is gradually losing momentum and becoming more vulnerable to a reversal.

The underlying logic is straightforward: if each new impulse wave attracts greater participation than the previous one, the trend is gaining strength and building momentum. Conversely, if each new impulse wave shows declining participation compared with the previous one, the trend is losing strength and approaching exhaustion, signaling that a potential shift in market structure may be approaching.

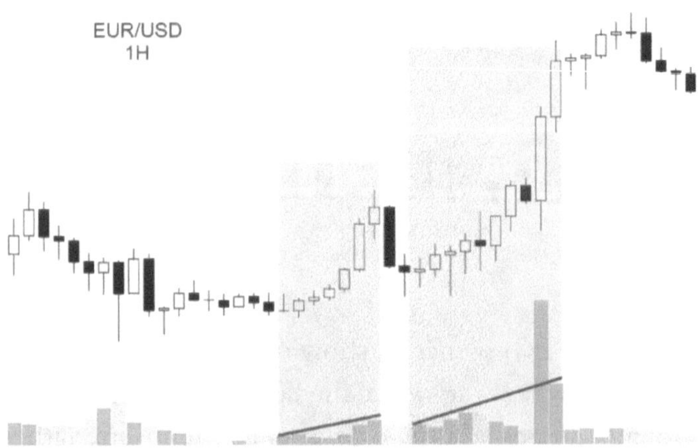

Figure 4.11: Example

Figure 4.11 demonstrates a real-market application of this method on the EUR/USD pair using the 1-hour timeframe. The chart shows a clear uptrend with two impulse waves highlighted on the chart. In both of these upward waves, volume exhibits a consistent rising pattern, indicating that participation is progressively strengthening.

You may also notice a noticeable volume spike in the data. This occurs during the session overlap between the European and U.S. trading sessions at around 10 AM EST—a period when volume surges are normal as two major sessions become active simultaneously. However, even if we ignore this spike and focus on the underlying pattern, it remains clear that volume is trending upward across both impulse waves.

When volume across waves moving in the same direction maintains or increases in this way, we can project with relatively high confidence that the uptrend still retains strength and has a strong probability of continuing in line with the current momentum.

Figure 4.12: Example

Figure 4.12 reveals what happened afterward. Price made a shallow pullback and then quickly rallied strongly, breaking above the most recent swing high and forming a new high. This move reflects an uptrend supported by increasing volume participation, demonstrating the effectiveness of volume analysis in anticipating trend continuation.

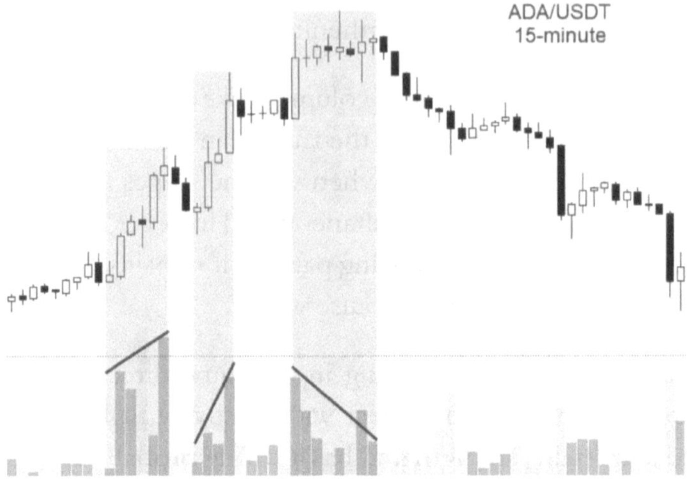

Figure 4.13: Example

Figure 4.13 demonstrates the second scenario—trend weakening through declining volume. The 15-minute chart of Cardano shows an uptrend consisting of three impulse waves. The first wave displays healthy volume progression, with volume gradually increasing, indicating strong buying participation. The second wave also shows rising volume, even steeper than the first, suggesting that the uptrend is accelerating.

However, the third wave is completely different—volume declines throughout the entire move while price continues to rise. This creates a clear divergence between price and volume.

This divergence pattern is a classic warning signal that the uptrend is losing strength and becoming vulnerable to reversal, and the subsequent price action confirms this expectation. A decline begins shortly after the third wave, with volume increasing during the downward moves, indicating that sellers are taking control decisively. Occasional recovery attempts appear, but they are all accompanied by extremely low volume, further confirming that buyers have largely exhausted their momentum.

Entering long positions in the zones following the third wave carries extremely high risk because it means trading alongside a trend that has already weakened significantly—an uptrend no longer supported by a solid volume foundation. Volume analysis provides an important early warning of trend deterioration before the reversal becomes obvious.

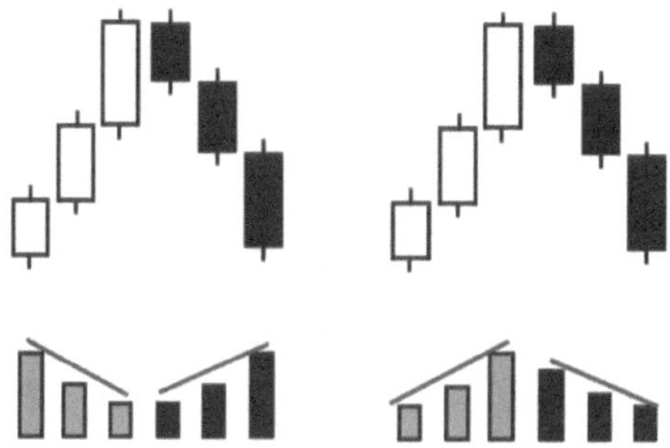

Figure 4.14: Price-Volume Correlation

In addition to comparing the volume of waves moving in the same direction, we can also apply a method that compares volume between impulse waves and corrective waves moving in opposite directions. This is an extremely powerful technique for identifying early reversal signals before they become obvious from price structure alone.

Figure 4.14 illustrates two contrasting scenarios within the context of an uptrend. The illustration on the left demonstrates a warning scenario: the upward wave (the impulse wave in the direction of the trend) shows progressively declining volume, while the downward wave (the corrective pullback against the trend) displays increasing volume. This inverse pattern reveals that sellers are gradually overwhelming buyers, participation is shifting from the bullish side to the bearish side, and the uptrend is losing conviction with a high probability of either reversing or entering a prolonged consolidation.

The illustration on the right demonstrates a healthy scenario. The upward wave (impulse) shows consistently increasing volume, while the downward wave (corrective) shows declining volume. This pattern confirms that buyers maintain firm control of the market—participation expands when price rallies in the direction of the trend, while pullbacks against the trend remain weak. As a result, the uptrend still has a solid foundation and is likely to continue.

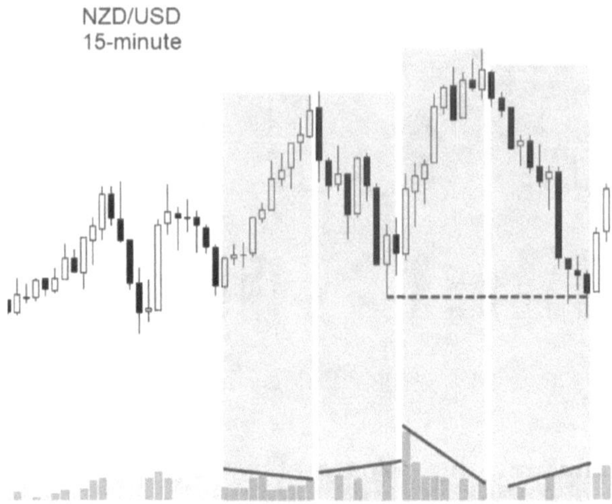

Figure 4.15: Example

Next, let us examine a real-market example of the first case—comparing the volume of waves moving in opposite directions. In this example, the NZD/USD pair is in the late stage of an uptrend.

The volume of the first upward wave already shows a gradual decline, although the slope of the decrease is not yet very pronounced. This serves as an early warning that the bullish momentum may be weakening. We can now compare the volume between waves moving in opposite directions. The first downward wave shows a slight increase in volume, suggesting that sellers are beginning to gain strength.

The second upward wave then delivers a much stronger warning signal. The volume associated with this wave declines with a steeper slope than the previous upward wave, clearly indicating weakening participation from buyers. At this point, it becomes evident that the uptrend has already lost much of its strength.

Next comes another downward wave, with volume rising more sharply than in the previous decline. This provides additional evidence that sellers are becoming increasingly dominant in the market.

If you trade without paying attention to volume, you might interpret this structure as a double bottom pattern. A double bottom is typically considered a bullish reversal pattern, and many traders would be inclined to enter long positions at this point.

However, once you incorporate volume analysis, the picture becomes very different. The volume behavior clearly shows that the prior uptrend has already weakened significantly. As a result, entering long positions here becomes highly risky, because the market no longer has the volume support needed to sustain a meaningful bullish move.

Figure 4.16: Example

In Figure 4.16, buyers attempt to push the price higher—representing a final effort from the bullish side. However, sellers quickly step in and drive the price down with a candle accompanied by very strong volume.

Do you see the implication here? This is a clear example of how analyzing the volume of waves moving in opposite directions can help anticipate shifts in market structure. The pattern itself may appear bullish, but volume reveals the underlying reality: sellers are in control of the market.

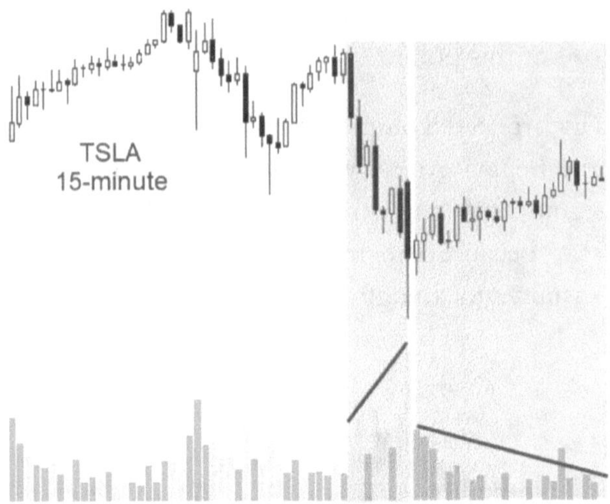

Figure 4.17: Example

Figure 4.17 presents Tesla stock on the 15-minute timeframe in a clear downtrend, characterized by lower highs and lower lows. The market displays a classic bearish structure. You can observe that the downward waves—the impulse waves moving in the direction of the trend—show volume that is either maintaining or progressively increasing, indicating that sellers remain active and aggressive. At the same time, the upward waves—the corrective moves against the trend—show consistently declining volume, revealing that buyers are weak and lack conviction. Based on this pattern analysis, we can project with relatively high confidence that the downtrend remains healthy and has a strong probability of continuing lower.

In the context of financial markets, recognizing this pattern has important practical implications. The purpose of the analysis here is not only to identify potential short opportunities, but also to avoid premature long entries. Reading this type of volume behavior tells us that entering long positions at the current price levels would be unwise, regardless of how temporarily attractive the price action might appear. Instead, patience is required.

We need to wait for a clear signal of structural change—specifically when the volume of the downward waves begins to show signs of exhaustion and decline, while the volume of the upward waves starts to increase significantly, signaling a potential shift in balance from sellers to buyers. Only when these signals appear can a new uptrend begin to establish itself. In the context of Figure 4.17, however, the most appropriate stance is to stay on the sidelines and observe—strictly avoiding long entries at the current price levels.

Figure 4.18: Example

Figure 4.18 reveals the subsequent development. Instead of reversing, price continues to decline sharply as projected, confirming the accuracy of the volume-based analysis. This serves as a clear demonstration of how volume analysis can protect traders from poor decisions—in this case, avoiding premature long positions during a strong downtrend helped prevent significant losses.

In summary, the three fundamental laws presented in this chapter—Supply and Demand, Cause and Effect, and Effort and Result—form the conceptual foundation of volume spread analysis. They are not isolated concepts but interconnected principles that reveal different aspects of market behavior. The Law of Supply and Demand explains why price moves. The Law of Cause and Effect explains the preparation phases behind major moves. The Law of Effort and Result provides real-time signals about the conviction behind price movements.

However, volume analysis alone represents only one side of the momentum equation. In the next chapter, we will explore how to identify the strength of buyers and sellers through direct analysis of price waves.

CHAPTER 5: WAVE MOMENTUM ANALYSIS

You have already mastered structural analysis in Chapter 2—the ability to identify swings, recognize reversals, and determine the direction of the trend. In Chapter 4, we explored the first part of momentum assessment through volume spread analysis, learning how to interpret effort–result relationships, supply–demand imbalances, and volume patterns to gauge the conviction behind a trend.

In this chapter, we move to the remaining component of momentum analysis, which lies within price action itself—specifically in the behavior and progression of waves. More precisely, we will evaluate trend strength through a systematic examination of impulse waves (waves moving in the direction of the trend) and corrective waves (waves moving against the trend).

We will explore four specific methods: comparing the expansion of impulse waves, analyzing the depth of corrective waves, examining the angle of waves, and evaluating slope changes within each wave. These methods provide early warnings of trend exhaustion or acceleration, allowing us to anticipate reversals and continuations before structural signals become obvious. Let us begin with a simple example below.

Figure 5.1: Price momentum

Figure 5.1 presents a simple yet powerful case study illustrating the importance of momentum analysis. The chart shows the EUR/USD pair on the 1-hour timeframe with two clearly distinct phases. The left half demonstrates a strong uptrend, with a series of higher highs and higher lows climbing steadily, creating the impression of a healthy and sustainable bullish trend. However, the right half reveals a completely different reality—price suddenly collapses in a sharp decline, catching traders off guard if they rely solely on structural signals.

So, is there a systematic method that allows us to anticipate dramatic reversals like this before they occur, rather than being surprised when the structure finally breaks? The answer lies in carefully analyzing the waves—both the impulse waves pushing in the direction of the trend and the corrective waves pulling against it—along with the relationships and progression patterns between them.

In the following sections, we will systematically explore methods for assessing the relationships between waves, learning how to recognize early warning signs of trend exhaustion.

Progression of Impulse Waves

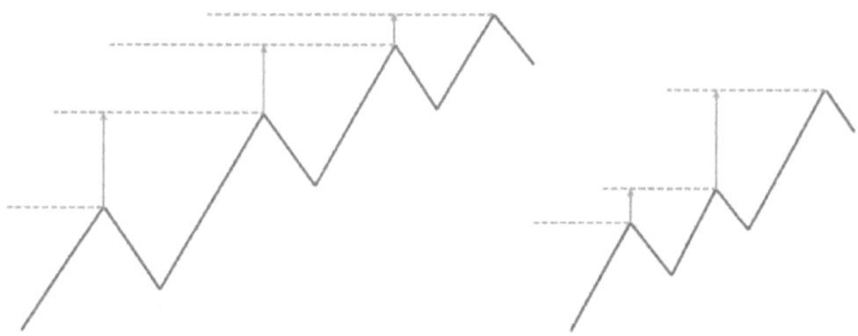

Figure 5.2: Strong vs Weak Price momentum

We begin with the first method—evaluating the progression of impulse waves to detect trend strength.

Figure 5.2 illustrates two scenarios of impulse wave progression. The illustration on the left shows a warning pattern. The distance between successive highs is progressively narrowing—the first wave produces a large gain, while each subsequent wave produces a smaller advance. This pattern reveals diminishing expansion, indicating that buyers no longer have the capacity to push price higher with the same intensity. As a result, the trend is approaching exhaustion and carries a high probability of reversing.

The illustration on the right shows a healthy pattern. The distance between the highs is expanding, with each wave traveling farther than the previous one. This behavior confirms that buyers maintain strong interest and increasing capacity, giving the trend a solid foundation to continue with accelerating momentum.

The logic behind this method is straightforward: if each impulse wave covers a greater distance than the previous one, the trend is gaining momentum. Conversely, if each wave travels a shorter distance, the trend is losing momentum and gradually moving closer to a potential reversal point.

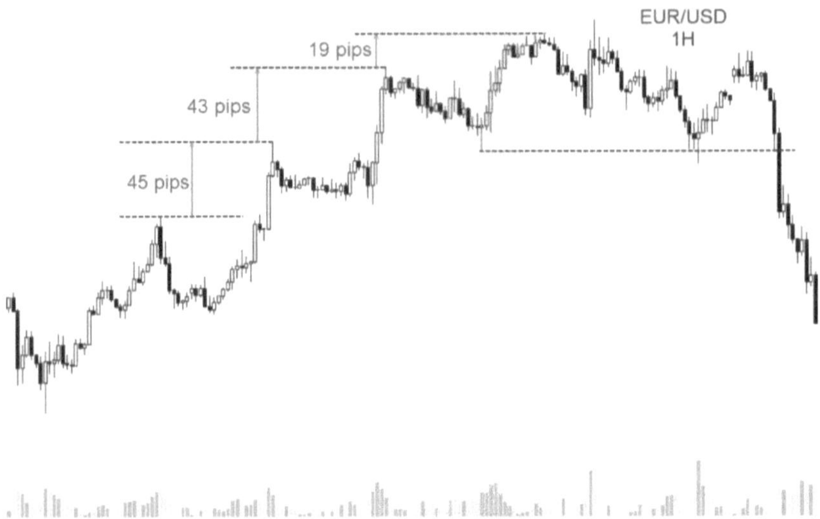

Figure 5.3: Price momentum

Now let us return to the previous example. Figure 5.3 demonstrates the application of this method on EUR/USD on the 1-hour timeframe. The measurements show a clear progression: the first wave travels 45 pips, the second wave 43 pips, and the third wave only 19 pips. This contraction pattern—where each wave becomes progressively weaker—reveals that buyers are losing both interest and the capacity to push price higher.

This pattern serves as a warning signal of momentum exhaustion. If traders consider long positions in the final area simply because the structure still appears intact, that decision carries significant risk, since the momentum analysis already indicates weakening strength. In this situation, the prudent stance is to avoid entering the market.

The subsequent price action validates this warning. Price declines sharply and breaks through the previous swing low, confirming the reversal.

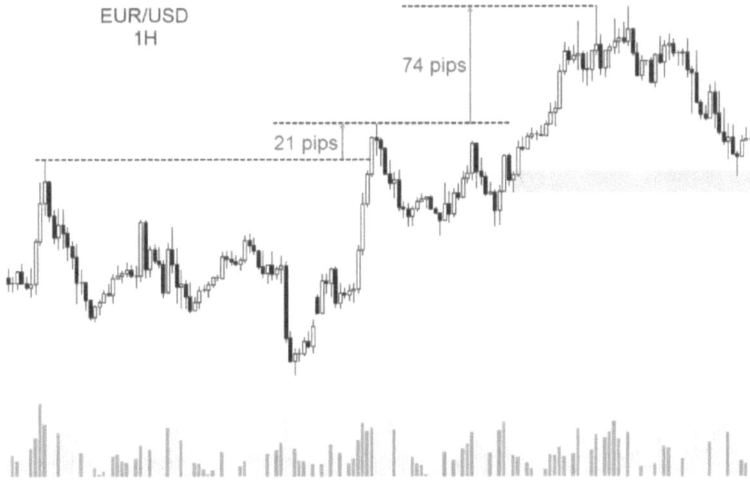

Figure 5.4: Example

Figure 5.4 presents the opposite scenario—an example of healthy momentum expansion within an uptrend. The EUR/USD 1-hour chart shows a pattern completely opposite to the earlier weakening example. The measurements reveal positive progression: the first impulse wave travels 21 pips, while the second expands to 74 pips—more than three times the distance of the previous wave. This expansion pattern—where each successive wave covers significantly more distance—confirms that buyers are not only maintaining interest but are also increasing participation and conviction in pushing price higher.

This pattern signals a sustainable uptrend with accelerating momentum. When price pulls back into the highlighted support zone, it becomes an attractive opportunity to consider long positions, as the momentum analysis clearly supports the likelihood of continuation.

Figure 5.5: Example

Figure 5.5 reveals what happens next. Price rallies strongly and breaks above the previous high, confirming that the analysis of expanding waves was correct. However, the new impulse wave measures only 56 pips, which is smaller than the 74 pips of the previous wave.

This marks a critical shift. After an expansion progression (from 21 to 74 pips), the current wave contracts to 56 pips. The structure remains bullish, but momentum analysis reveals that the rate of expansion has slowed. This serves as an early warning that buyers may be losing steam, and traders should exercise caution with new long positions.

Figure 5.6: Example

Figure 5.6 reveals the outcome of the momentum warning. Price declines sharply and breaks below the swing low, confirming that the uptrend has been exhausted and has entered a correction. This pattern demonstrates why contracting impulse waves are so important—they provide advance notice before the structure actually breaks.

If we also observe the volume in this example, we can see that the volume during the final rally attempts is declining, as illustrated in the chart. This further reinforces the assessment that buyers are weakening.

Depth of Corrective Waves

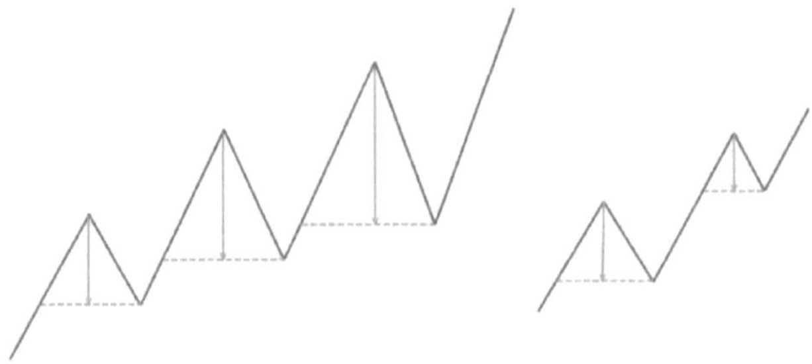

Figure 5.7: Strong vs Weak Price Momentum

In addition to assessing impulse waves, we can also analyze the depth of corrective waves to gauge the health of a trend.

Figure 5.7 illustrates two scenarios. The illustration on the left shows a warning pattern. The corrective waves become progressively deeper—the first pullback is shallow, the second is deeper, and the third becomes even deeper. This pattern reveals that sellers are gaining strength and pushing price lower with increasing force. As a result, buyers are gradually losing control, and the uptrend becomes vulnerable to a potential reversal.

The illustration on the right shows a healthy pattern. The depth of the corrective waves progressively decreases, with each pullback becoming shallower than the previous one. This behavior confirms that sellers lack the strength to push price significantly lower, while buyers maintain control and quickly absorb selling pressure. Under these conditions, the uptrend has strong conviction and is more likely to continue.

This is a powerful analytical tool. In a healthy uptrend, pullbacks should generally become progressively shallower, confirming that buyers dominate the market and are willing to step in at increasingly higher levels. In contrast, deepening pullbacks signal that sellers are gradually gaining ground.

Figure 5.8: Example

Figure 5.8 demonstrates corrective wave depth analysis on Solana on the 1-hour timeframe. The measurements show a concerning progression: the first corrective wave retraces 42 pips, the second deepens to 65 pips (an increase of more than 50%), and the third deteriorates further to 82 pips. This progressively deepening pattern forms a clear trend of expanding retracements.

This pattern serves as a warning signal. It reveals that sellers are systematically gaining strength and pushing price deeper with each cycle, while buyers are losing the ability to defend higher levels. The evidence becomes even more compelling when we examine the price action after the 82-pip pullback: buyers are nearly absent—volume is extremely low—showing little enthusiasm to push price higher. As a result, price declines sharply.

This example demonstrates the predictive power of momentum analysis. By observing the pattern of deepening pullbacks, this method provides advance warning of underlying weakness, signaling traders to avoid long positions or exit existing trades before a major decline occurs.

Angle of Impulse Waves

Figure 5.9: Momentum - Impulse Angle

Next, we explore another important dimension—comparing the angle of impulse waves to evaluate whether price is more likely to reverse or continue its trend.

Figure 5.9 illustrates this concept. Impulse waves are measured not only by distance but also by their steepness. The first wave has a steep angle, reflecting strong upward momentum. The second wave becomes less steep, suggesting that buying pressure is already losing some of its aggressiveness. By the third impulse wave, the slope has flattened significantly—it is the flattest of the three waves—indicating that buyers have clearly weakened. At this point, traders should exercise great caution with new long positions.

Conversely, if the impulse waves become progressively steeper, this indicates that buyers are growing more aggressive, and the uptrend has a higher probability of continuing.

The angle of ascent or descent is a visual representation of momentum. Steep angles indicate strong, aggressive momentum, while flatter angles suggest weak, sluggish momentum. This makes angle analysis a quick and effective visual assessment tool.

Figure 5.10: Momentum - Impulse Angle

Figure 5.10 demonstrates angle analysis on Amazon on the daily timeframe. The trend lines drawn along the impulse waves reveal progressive deceleration. The first wave is steep and aggressive, the second wave becomes noticeably flatter—showing that the rate of ascent is slowing—and the third wave is the flattest, with price barely progressing along a shallow trajectory.

This pattern of flattening angles serves as a visual warning of exhaustion. When the final impulse wave (wave four) completes, price breaks below the two previous swing lows in a major breakdown, accompanied by a surge in volume. This confirms that sellers have taken control while buyers have become exhausted. The subsequent decline pushes price back close to the starting point of the uptrend.

This example demonstrates the predictive capability of momentum analysis. The visual cue of progressively flattening angles provides an unmistakable warning that momentum is draining from the trend, allowing prudent traders to exit positions or prepare for a potential reversal before the market structure ultimately collapses.

Angle of Corrective Waves

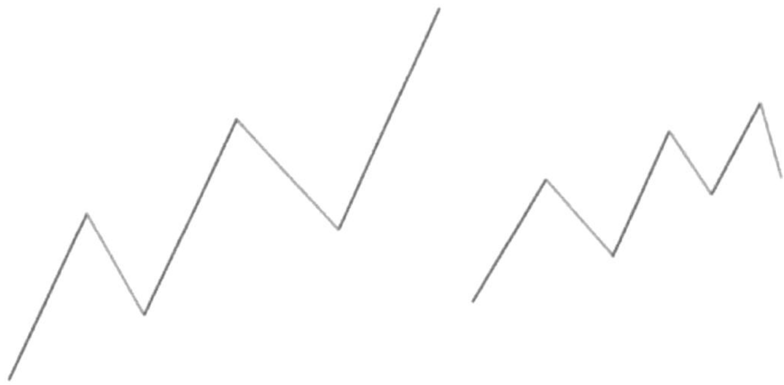

Figure 5.11: Price Momentum - Corrective Wave Angle

In addition to impulse waves, we can apply the same principle of angle analysis to corrective waves to assess the balance of power in the market.

Figure 5.11 illustrates two scenarios. The illustration on the left shows a healthy pattern. The angles of the corrective waves gradually flatten—the first pullback is moderate, while the second becomes shallower. This pattern reveals that the countertrend forces (sellers) are weakening, while buyers maintain control, giving the uptrend a solid foundation to continue.

The illustration on the right shows a warning pattern. The angles progressively steepen—the first pullback is gentle, the second becomes steeper, and the third is steeper still. This indicates that the countertrend forces are gaining strength, with sellers becoming increasingly aggressive and pushing price lower with accelerating momentum. It serves as a warning signal that the balance of power may be shifting, making the trend vulnerable to a potential reversal.

Now let us look at a real chart example of the NZD/USD pair below.

Figure 5.12: Momentum - Example

Figure 5.12 demonstrates corrective angle analysis on NZD/USD on the 1-hour timeframe during an uptrend. The trend lines drawn along the corrective waves (down waves) reveal a significant pattern. The first wave shows a moderate and relatively aggressive descent. The second wave becomes noticeably flatter, indicating that the rate of decline has slowed. This flattening pattern continues in the subsequent corrections.

Flattening corrective angles are a bullish signal. They reveal that sellers are losing strength with each attempt and are no longer able to push price downward with the same intensity as before. Buyers remain in control and quickly absorb selling pressure, preventing deep pullbacks.

When price pulls back to the highlighted support level, this becomes a high-probability long opportunity with a favorable risk-reward profile. Momentum analysis confirms the health of the uptrend and suggests a continuation. The subsequent price action validates this expectation: price resumes its upward movement and establishes a new swing high, confirming that the trend strength remains intact.

Figure 5.13: Momentum - Example

Figure 5.13 demonstrates how steepening corrective waves can signal a reversal. The left half of the chart presents Bank of America on the 4-hour timeframe during a downtrend. The trend lines drawn along the corrective waves (rallies) reveal a progressive pattern.

The first wave has a flat and weak angle, with buyers making minimal progress. The second and third waves become progressively steeper, indicating that the rate of ascent is accelerating. By the fourth wave, the steepening becomes dramatic, with an angle approaching vertical, and price breaks decisively above the previous swing high. This represents a structural breakthrough accompanied by a clear shift in momentum.

This steepening pattern is a powerful reversal warning. It reveals that buyers are systematically gaining strength with each attempt, gradually overwhelming sellers and preparing to take control of the market. The subsequent price action confirms this interpretation: price continues to rally in a sustained move and breaks sequentially above prior highs, establishing a new uptrend and validating the prediction.

Slope of the Wave

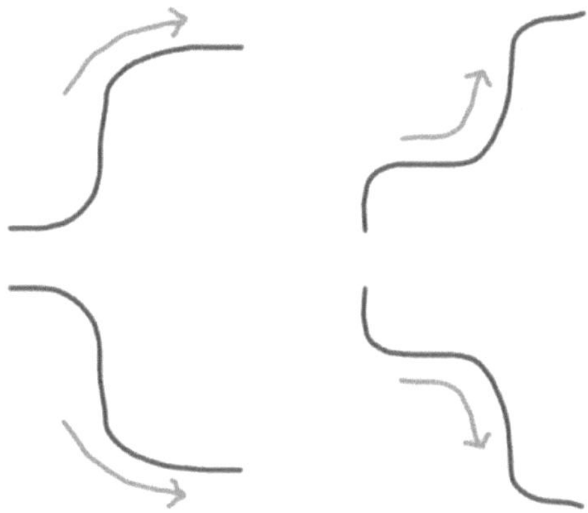

Figure 5.14: Momentum - Slope

Finally, we examine a more detailed dimension—analyzing slope changes within individual waves to reveal intra-wave momentum shifts.

Figure 5.14 illustrates four scenarios of slope behavior. Imagine climbing a mountain—the slope reveals how momentum evolves over time.

The top-left scenario (upward deceleration) shows a rally that begins steep but gradually flattens as it approaches the high, transitioning from a strong climb into a sideways movement. It is similar to climbing uphill and then reaching a plateau. This deceleration reveals that buyers are losing steam and that momentum is weakening.

The top-right scenario (sustained acceleration) shows a wave that maintains its steepness from the low to the high. The slope remains consistently steep without flattening, like a continuous uphill climb. This confirms that strong momentum is persisting.

The bottom-left scenario (downward deceleration) shows a decline that starts steep but gradually flattens as it approaches the low. The downward movement slows, similar to descending a hill and then leveling off. This suggests that sellers are losing conviction and may be approaching exhaustion.

The bottom-right scenario (sustained descent) shows a decline that remains steep throughout the entire wave, reflecting consistently aggressive selling pressure. It resembles a straight downhill path and indicates strong bearish momentum with no clear signs of exhaustion.

The key insight is that slope flattening within waves signals fading momentum and a potential reversal, while sustained slopes indicate continuing strength in the current move.

Figure 5.15: Momentum - Example

Figure 5.15 demonstrates intra-wave slope analysis on Binance Coin on the 15-minute timeframe. Curved lines trace two decline waves, revealing critical differences between them.

The first decline wave maintains a steep downward slope from peak to trough. The angle remains aggressive throughout the entire move, indicating strong selling pressure. Sellers are firmly in control, reflecting healthy bearish momentum.

The second wave is fundamentally different. It begins with a steep descent but progressively flattens as it approaches the low. The movement transitions from an aggressive decline into a more horizontal trajectory, revealing that sellers are losing momentum and can no longer maintain the same level of pressure.

Slope flattening at the extremity serves as an early reversal warning. It suggests that exhaustion is occurring within the wave itself, even before structural signals appear. The subsequent price action confirms this interpretation: price reverses and rallies strongly. Recognizing slope deceleration can therefore provide advance notice of potential reversals before they become obvious on the chart.

Figure 5.16: Momentum - Example

Figure 5.16 presents USD/JPY on the 1-hour timeframe demonstrating slope analysis. A curved line traces two impulse waves, revealing clear differences in their slopes.

The first wave maintains a steep upward slope from the low to the high. The angle remains aggressive throughout the entire move, indicating strong buying momentum. Buyers push price upward with conviction, forming a healthy bullish impulse wave.

The second wave, however, becomes problematic. It begins with a steep ascent but progressively flattens as it approaches the peak instead of maintaining its aggressive angle. The movement transitions from a steep climb into a more horizontal trajectory before reaching the high. This premature flattening signals that buyers are losing momentum within the rally.

This is a practical example of slope-based prediction. When a rally fails to maintain a steep angle all the way to the peak and instead flattens prematurely, it provides an advance warning that momentum is weakening—even if price is still making new highs. The subsequent price action shows a reversal, validating the warning signal.

Thus, the four methods in this chapter—impulse progression, corrective depths, wave angles, and intra-wave slopes—together with the momentum analysis through volume discussed in Chapter 4, form a complete toolkit for assessing momentum without relying on noisy indicators.

Expanding impulse waves with shallowing pullbacks signal healthy acceleration. Contracting impulses with deepening corrections warn that exhaustion may be approaching. Steepening angles confirm strengthening momentum, while flattening slopes within waves reveal real-time deterioration.

These methods transform the way you read trends. Instead of waiting for structural breaks to confirm reversals, you gain advance warnings through progressively weakening signals. Instead of hoping that rallies will continue, you obtain objective evidence of sustainability through wave-quality metrics. This is the difference between reactive trading and proactive trading.

In the next chapter, we will explore an entry technique used by the composite trader—known as **Testing**.

CHAPTER 6: TESTING – THE ART OF THE COMPOSITE MAN

In this chapter, we come to a concept that is extremely critical in momentum analysis—Testing. Many traders are familiar with the idea of a "retest": when price breaks above a high, pulls back to retest that level, and then continues to rally if the test holds; or when price breaks below a low, retests it, and then continues to decline.

Testing in the context of Volume Spread Analysis shares some similarities with the retest concept, but it is fundamentally broader and much deeper.

Testing is not simply price returning to a level. It is a deliberate process through which the market verifies the balance of supply and demand at critical zones before committing to a directional move. It is an essential step that marks the moments when the market prepares to transition into a new phase—whether from accumulation to markup, from distribution to markdown, or from consolidation into a trending phase.

The importance of testing cannot be overstated. It is the missing piece that explains why some retests succeed spectacularly while others fail miserably, even though the surface-level price action may appear very similar.

Definition of Testing

Testing is a necessary verification step that the market conducts to confirm whether a trend has the foundation to continue or whether a reversal has sufficient conviction to establish itself. This process reveals critical information about the underlying supply–demand dynamics—information that cannot be obtained when price is simply moving freely.

The key principle is straightforward: a test on high volume suggests that price may continue moving in the same direction as the testing wave, whereas a test on low volume indicates that the testing pressure is being absorbed by the opposing side. In the latter scenario, support or resistance continues to function as an effective barrier, increasing the likelihood that price will move in the opposite direction of the testing wave.

This is a critical distinction that the majority of traders can miss when they focus only on price action. Understanding this distinction can transform your ability to predict post-test behavior with dramatically higher accuracy.

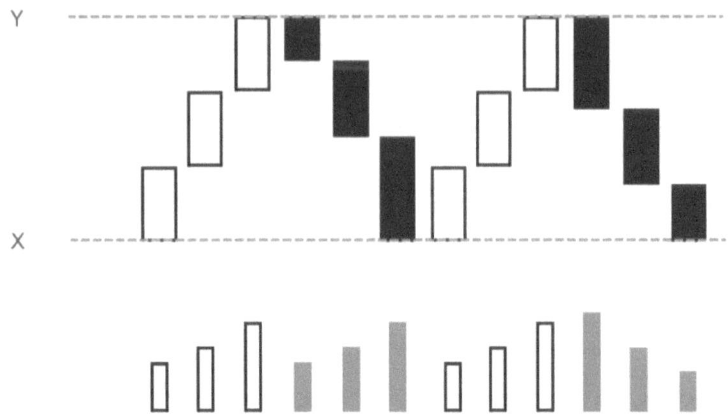

Figure 6.1: Price and Volume

To truly understand why testing is critical, we need to think like smart money—participants with large capital and long-term strategic objectives. Let us walk through a specific scenario.

Figure 6.1 illustrates a simple but revealing uptrend scenario. Suppose we are a smart-money institution with the objective of accumulating positions at zone X (a lower support level) and subsequently pushing price toward target Y (a higher resistance level). On the journey from X to Y, we will encounter two fundamental categories of obstacles that must be overcome in order to achieve this objective.

Obstacle One – Early Buyers Taking Profits: Traders who bought alongside us at zone X or nearby are now sitting on unrealized gains. As we progressively push price upward, their natural psychological reaction is to lock in profits—they will sell to realize those gains. Each sell order from these early buyers creates supply that we—holding long positions and aiming for higher prices—must absorb if we want the rally to continue. If we refuse to absorb this selling pressure, price will stall or decline, preventing us from reaching target Y.

Obstacle Two – Floating Supply from Prior Distribution: At level Y and in the zones above it, there is existing supply from traders who bought at higher prices in the past and are now trapped or waiting for a break-even opportunity to exit. As price rallies toward Y, these participants see a chance to escape their losses or reduce their positions, so they begin selling aggressively. Similarly, when price attempts to push above Y, additional sellers may emerge from even higher levels. This is known as floating supply—existing positions waiting for an opportunity to liquidate—and it represents the second obstacle, potentially a massive one, blocking the path upward.

Now consider the situation from the perspective of smart money. The volume panel in Figure 6.1 shows tall bars during the rally attempts, indicating heavy selling pressure from both early profit-takers and floating supply. The critical question is this: would you want to spend significant capital right now to absorb all of that selling volume in a single aggressive push? Or would you prefer a smarter and more capital-efficient approach—waiting for price to test these levels again with low volume, confirming that sellers have been exhausted, before committing capital to a sustained markup phase?

The answer is clear: smart money always chooses patience. They wait for low-volume tests that confirm supply depletion before committing to aggressive accumulation and the subsequent markup phase.

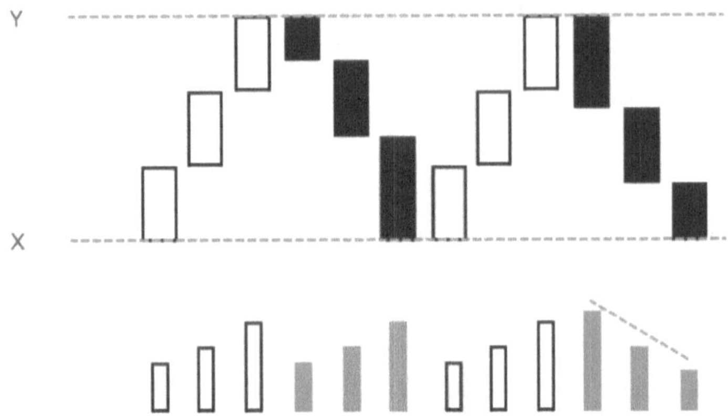

Figure 6.2: Price and Volume

That is the true meaning behind testing. When smart money pushes price and absorbs floating supply until it dries up—until there are no meaningful sellers left—the subsequent upward push will encounter minimal resistance. The path is cleared. Each unit of capital now translates into more efficient price movement. The more cost-efficient the path becomes, the more profit margins are maximized.

Wave Testing

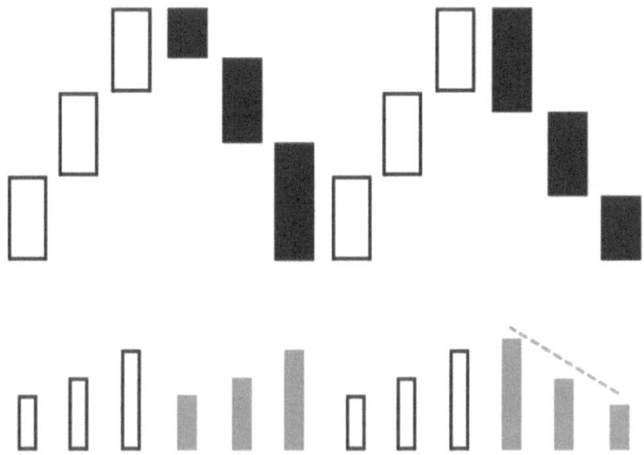

Figure 6.3: Wave Testing

Within the scope of this book, we focus on Wave Testing—a systematic approach to identifying tests through corrective wave behavior.

Figure 6.3 illustrates the mechanics in an uptrend. After the first impulse wave with increasing volume, we monitor the subsequent corrective wave pulling back toward support. The critical point is that this testing wave must show declining volume, as illustrated by the downward trend line in the volume panel.

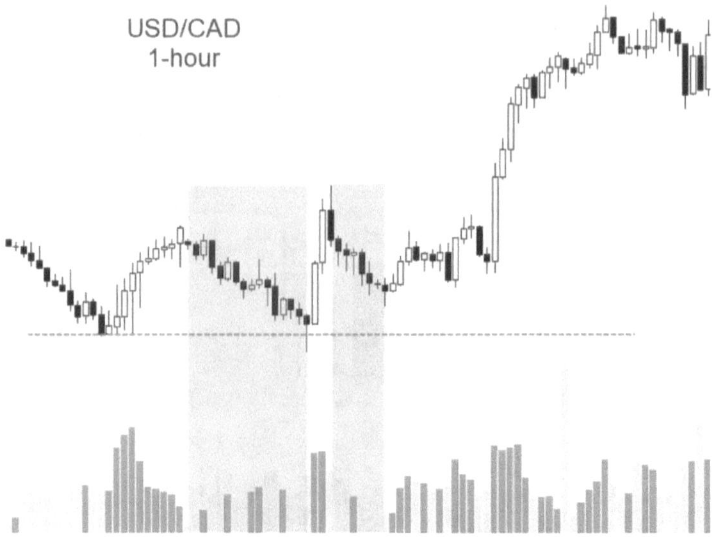

Figure 6.4: Wave Testing - Example

Figure 6.4 demonstrates wave testing on USD/CAD on the 1-hour timeframe, with two corrective waves highlighted, allowing us to compare their volume characteristics across cycles.

First Corrective Wave: The volume panel reveals high bars, indicating heavy selling pressure as price pulls back toward support. This high volume signals that significant supply is still actively present—including floating sellers exiting positions and early buyers taking profits. This is considered a failed test because too much supply remains in the market, showing that the market is not yet ready for a sustained rally.

Second Corrective Wave – Successful Test: After the rally is rejected, the market declines again, but with a critical difference. Volume is dramatically lower compared to the previous wave, revealing that selling pressure has been fundamentally depleted. More importantly, price does not reach the prior support level and instead stops higher, demonstrating that sellers are no longer willing to push price down aggressively. This combined pattern—low volume together with the failure to penetrate the previous lows—confirms that supply has been absorbed.

This low-volume test, coupled with the inability to reach support validates a successful verification of supply depletion. The subsequent price action proves the accuracy of the signal: the market explodes into a powerful rally. With supply verified as absent, the setup becomes a high-probability long opportunity.

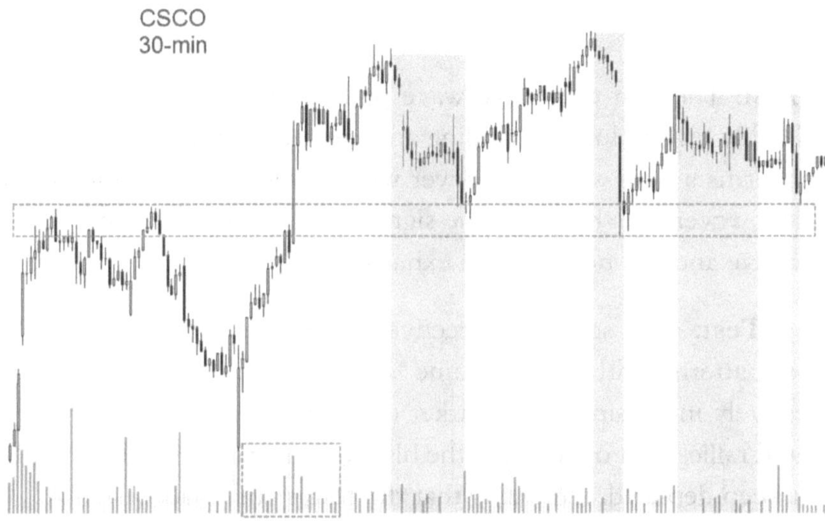

Figure 6.5: Wave Testing - Example

Figure 6.5 presents a classic testing case that clearly demonstrates the persistence of the testing process. The chart shows Cisco stock on the 30-minute timeframe with multiple test attempts at a key support zone, providing a perfect example of why patience is critical in the wave testing methodology.

Context Setup: Before analyzing the tests, first identify the uptrend structure with two prior swing highs that create a resistance zone, marked by the upper horizontal line. After price breaks decisively above this resistance, the zone transforms into a support area—old highs become new support according to structural principles. This is the level we want to monitor for potential testing opportunities.

Testing Criterion: To enter long positions at this former high area with confidence, we need to see price pull back to the support zone accompanied by low volume, confirming supply exhaustion. However, to properly assess whether the volume in the corrective waves is "high" or "low," we must first establish a baseline by comparing it with the preceding opposite-direction wave, marked by the dotted rectangle. That wave exhibits moderate volume, which serves as the reference point for our comparisons.

First Test: The first corrective wave pulls back to support but exhibits considerably high volume, including an extremely large volume spike. The market forms a base with long lower wicks indicating rejection, and then rallies. However, this high volume signals a failed test—too much supply is still active and has not yet been exhausted.

Second Test: The second corrective wave also demonstrates a high-volume pattern, with the volume bars of the component candles progressively increasing. The market once again forms a base with long wicks and rallies. But once again, the high volume confirms that supply has not yet been depleted, indicating that the test is still unsuccessful.

As emphasized earlier, when price retests a level with high volume, the subsequent rallies tend to be only temporary moves because supply has not yet been cleared. The market must continue testing until a corrective wave appears with truly low volume, confirming exhaustion. This process may require four, five, or even six test attempts—as long as the final corrective wave exhibits the low-volume verification needed to confirm that supply has been absorbed.

Third Test – Finally Successful: Only by the third corrective wave does the pattern fundamentally shift. This wave demonstrates markedly lower volume compared with the two prior tests, and critically, the volume of its component candles progressively decreases rather than increases. This declining volume progression reveals that the selling force has substantially weakened—bears have become significantly exhausted through the successive testing cycles. This is the confirmation signal that the correction phase is approaching completion and that the supply-testing process has finally concluded successfully. With the low-volume test verified, the path upward is cleared. Let us now observe how price moves next.

Figure 6.6: Wave Testing - Example

Figure 6.6 reveals the dramatic outcome following the successful completion of the low-volume test. After price successfully concludes the supply-testing process through the third corrective wave—with declining volume confirming that the selling force has been fundamentally exhausted and that bears no longer have the capacity to push price lower—bulls now have a clear path to initiate a sustained markup phase. The subsequent price action demonstrates the textbook result of proper testing verification: the market explodes into a powerful, sustained rally, illustrated by the ascending trend line, climbing substantially higher with minimal resistance encountered.

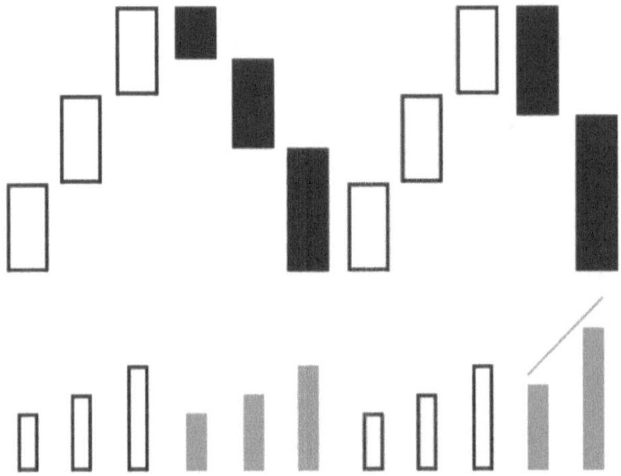

Figure 6.7: Testing - High Volume

Figure 6.7 illustrates the high-volume test pattern in an uptrend. When a corrective wave pulls back to support with high or increasing volume, this is not a confirmation of a successful test but rather a warning signal. High volume reveals that significant supply is still active—sellers remain eager to distribute, and resistance has not yet been cleared.

The market may evolve in one of two ways. First, it may continue retesting the level until a low-volume test eventually appears, as seen in the CISCO example with multiple attempts. Second, if the tests repeatedly occur with high volume—particularly when volume progressively increases—this indicates that supply remains too strong, and price is more likely to continue moving in the direction of the testing wave .

Let us now look at the example below.

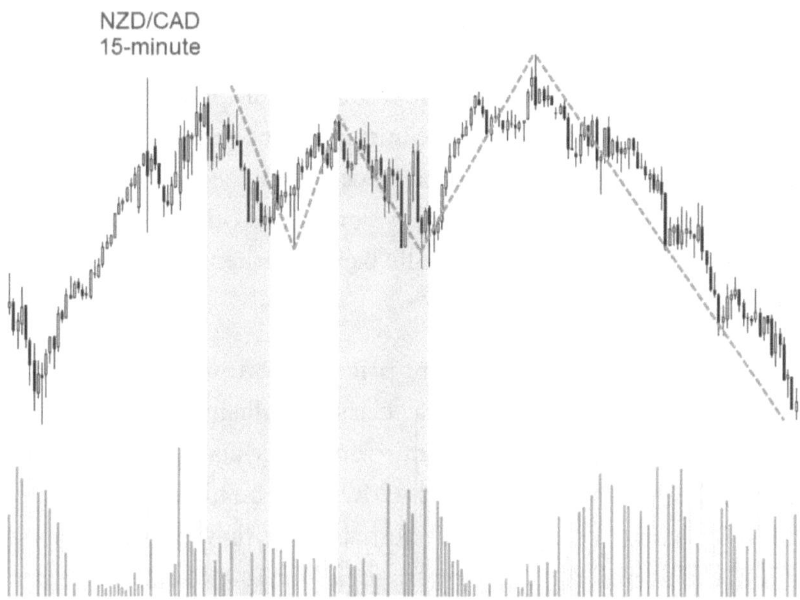

Figure 6.8: Wave Testing - Example

Figure 6.8 illustrates the importance of volume analysis during the testing process using the NZD/CAD 15-minute chart, providing a cautionary example of the dangers of ignoring high-volume signals. The chart shows an overall uptrend context, but with warning signs emerging during the testing phases, demonstrating why distinguishing volume characteristics is essential.

Context Analysis: The market had previously been in an uptrend, but the most recent impulse wave—although covering a considerable distance—was not accompanied by correspondingly strong volume, creating the first warning sign of potential momentum weakness. After this wave, the market entered a corrective phase with two pullback attempts highlighted.

First Corrective Wave: Price rallied briefly but encountered supply and declined. The key observation is that the selling volume during this corrective wave was significantly higher than the volume of the preceding upward wave, indicating that supply was entering the market aggressively and overpowering the previous buying pressure. This represents a failed test—too much supply remains active.

Second Corrective Wave: The next rally attempt shows even higher volume than the first wave, with selling pressure intensifying rather than diminishing. This pattern—progressively increasing volume across successive tests—is a major red flag. It signals not only that supply has not been exhausted but that it may actually be strengthening, suggesting a high probability of a trend reversal.

Many traders who focus only on price action would recognize this structure as a double bottom—a classic bullish reversal pattern in traditional technical analysis—and enter long positions without considering the volume implications. However, the high volume within the corrective waves warns that supply remains strongly present, making the pattern unreliable and the entry premature. Without volume confirmation showing that supply has been exhausted, trading such patterns becomes highly vulnerable to traps.

Subsequent price action validates the volume analysis. The market does rally temporarily after the second wave—but recall the principle: when tests occur with high volume, subsequent rallies tend to be **only temporary** because supply has not been cleared. After this brief rise, price reverses decisively and breaks sharply below the support area with continued high volume, driving through both lows of the supposed double bottom pattern. Traders who entered long positions based solely on the price pattern without volume confirmation were trapped and stopped out. The double bottom failed precisely because the high-volume tests had already warned that supply remained present rather than exhausted.

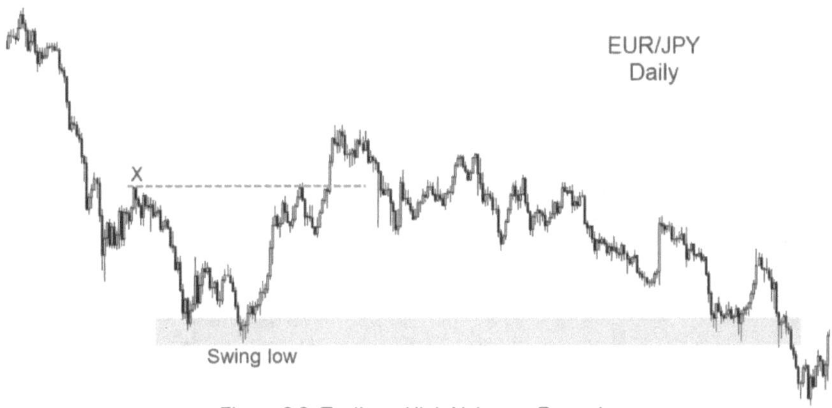

Figure 6.9: Testing - High Volume - Example

Figure 6.9 presents an important case study of high-volume testing on the EUR/JPY daily chart, illustrating price behavior in the context of a structural reversal.

The market had been in a prolonged downtrend until price broke above resistance level X, shifting the structure into a potential uptrend. The marked swing low represents the launching point of this breakout move.

After the breakout and the establishment of the new structure, observe the right side of the chart as price pulls back to test the swing low zone—now transformed into support. The critical question is: what happens to volume during this pullback? To clearly observe the volume behavior, we need to examine a zoomed-out view of the volume panel, as shown in **Figure 6.10**.

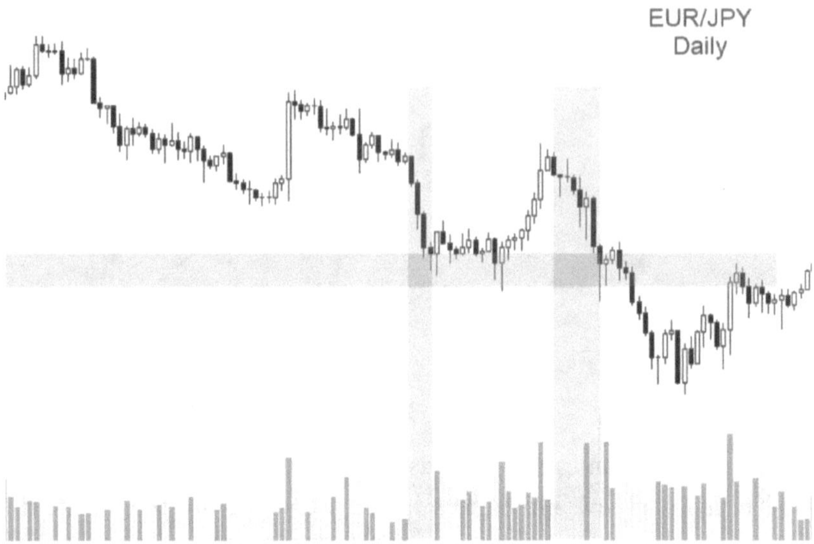

Figure 6.10: Testing - High Volume - Example

Figure 6.10 reveals the full testing process with the volume panel visible, allowing us to compare the characteristics of the two tests.

First Test – Low Volume: When price first pulls back to the support level, volume is low, indicating that selling pressure is diminishing and supply has been largely exhausted. This represents a successful test—there are no aggressive sellers left in the market. Traders may consider entering long positions with the expectation that the trend will continue, and the subsequent rally validates this setup. If a long position is taken at the first test, partial profits can be secured once the rally reaches twice the initial risk, locking in gains while reducing exposure.

Second Test – High Volume: Price later pulls back to the support level again (the rectangle on the right), but this time the volume is dramatically higher and increasing. Should traders buy here? **No.** High volume is a clear red flag—supply remains aggressive, making this test fundamentally different from the first one.

If traders are still holding positions from the first test, the correct response when witnessing this high-volume retest is to exit immediately to protect profits or minimize potential losses. This is not a continuation signal but rather a warning of a possible reversal.

When to Re-enter: A new entry should only be considered if another retest occurs with low volume, confirming that supply has finally been exhausted. If volume continues to appear high during the retest, the prudent decision is to stay out of the market.

After the second high-volume test, price declines sharply, breaking below the support level. The market reverses from an uptrend into a downtrend, perfectly validating why high-volume retests should be treated as warning signals.

When a pullback occurs with high volume, it often carries a sense of underlying pressure in the market. A low-volume retest is generally acceptable, while a high-volume retest is a clear warning. This distinction is fundamental, and mastering it can dramatically improve trade timing. As this example shows, testing analysis not only helps traders identify high-quality entries to follow a trend, but also protects them from obvious losing trades. Avoiding losing trades is, in many ways, just as valuable as capturing winning ones.

Thus, we have reached the end of Chapter 6. Testing is the missing link that explains why some trades succeed while others fail. The core insight is simple: smart money does not commit capital to moves that have not been verified. Instead, they systematically test the market to confirm that opposing forces have been exhausted before acting.

The patience to wait for low-volume confirmations instead of chasing moves prematurely is what separates disciplined traders from those who become trapped. When you see the market test a level multiple times—such as in the CISCO example, where the first test shows high volume, the second test still shows high volume, and only the third test finally appears with low volume—do not interpret this as weakness or indecision in the trend. It is simply the natural process the market must go through to systematically clear out remaining supply or demand at that level. Each high-volume test absorbs another portion of the opposing pressure until it is finally exhausted. Your job is to observe the volume signatures that reveal when the testing process has truly been completed—not to predict how many tests it will take.

Chapter 6 therefore serves as an essential complement to Chapter 2 (Market Structure), Chapter 4 (Volume), and Chapter 5 (Wave Momentum), helping you further refine your analytical and trading skill set. But even that is not enough. In the next chapter, we will add another powerful skill that will bring you closer to identifying high-probability entry points.

And this is likely something you have been waiting for.

Let's continue with Chapter 7 – Candlestick Analysis with Volume.

CHAPTER 7: CANDLESTICK ANALYSIS WITH VOLUME

By this point, we have built a solid foundation through the previous six chapters by learning how to identify market structure and assess market momentum. Chapter 7 serves as the bridge between M (Momentum) and T (Trigger)—but in a slightly different form.

In the earlier chapters, we analyzed the relationship between price waves and volume. In this final theoretical chapter, we will continue to focus on volume, but through a more microscopic lens—examining individual candlesticks in relation to their volume.

In other words, we will zoom in on the candles to look for the final clues that reveal when one side of the market has run out of energy and the other side is preparing to take control.

Mastering the techniques in this chapter means you are finally ready to execute trades with confidence.

Let's begin this systematic journey through candlestick–volume analysis.

Analyzing Candlestick Types in Relation to Volume

We begin with a critical foundation: understanding candlesticks not only through price structure but through their integration with volume, which reveals deeper truths about the underlying supply–demand dynamics.

Most traders analyze candlesticks based on price formations alone—pin bars signaling rejection, engulfing patterns indicating reversals, or Marubozu candles suggesting strong conviction. This standard methodology certainly has value, but it remains incomplete because it ignores the volume dimension.

As discussed in Chapter 4, the Effort–Result Principle states that effort (volume) should correspond with the result (price movement). Previously, we applied this concept at the wave level. Now we drill down to the level of individual candlesticks, examining whether a candle's price action is properly supported by the corresponding volume. This shift allows for a far more precise identification of potential entry and exit points.

When analyzing the relationship between candlesticks and volume, three fundamental scenarios can emerge, each revealing distinctly different market conditions and implications. Understanding these scenarios transforms chart reading from simple surface observation into a deeper form of market intelligence.

In the following sections, we will systematically explore each of these scenarios.

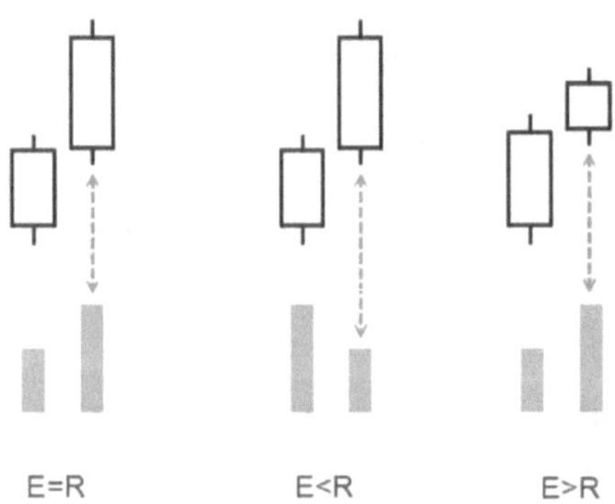

Figure 7.1: Effort & Result

Three Types of Candles Based on Volume Relationship

First, we will examine candlestick types through their relationship with volume.

Figure 7.1 presents a fundamental classification of candlesticks based on the relationship between price movement (result) and volume (effort), establishing a systematic framework for advanced VSA analysis. For clarity, the examples are illustrated within an uptrend context, but the same principles apply equally to downtrend scenarios with the interpretations appropriately inverted.

There are three primary types of candles.

The first type is the synchronized candle, where price and volume move in alignment—referred to as E = R (Effort = Result).

The remaining candles are non-synchronized, meaning the relationship between price movement and volume is imbalanced. These can be divided into two distinct subtypes.

The first subtype is E < R—a candle with low volume but a large spread, meaning low effort produces a large result.

The second subtype is E > R—a candle with high volume but a small spread, meaning high effort produces a small result.

Let's now examine each of these candle types in detail.

E < R Pattern

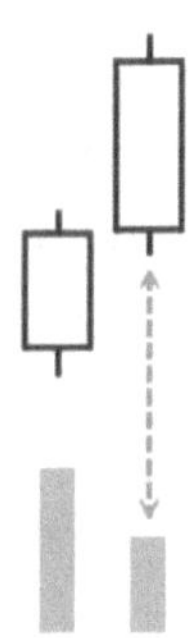

Figure 7.2: Effort < Result

Figure 7.2 illustrates the E < R pattern. Two candles show expanding upward bodies, yet the second volume bar is lower than the first (indicated by the downward arrow). This represents a textbook E < R condition—low effort producing a high result.

Bullish Candle – FOMO Buying: When E < R appears on a rallying candle, as shown in Figure 7.2—a large upward body accompanied by declining volume—it signals FOMO-driven buying. Retail traders chase the price aggressively, afraid of missing the rally. Although the price movement appears substantial, participation is weakening, revealing the absence of strong backing from smart money. What remains is primarily late-stage retail enthusiasm, which often occurs near the exhaustion phase of a move.

Bearish Candle – Panic Selling: When E < R appears on a declining candle—a large downward body with decreasing volume—it reflects panic selling. Price drops sharply, yet the volume remains relatively low, suggesting that the move is not driven by systematic distribution but rather by emotionally driven retail liquidation. Smart money is typically absent in these situations, having already exited earlier or preparing to accumulate positions.

The absence of smart money participation makes E < R conditions extremely prone to reversal. Such candles violate the Effort–Result Principle, creating unstable price levels that are vulnerable to corrections. A large price movement accompanied by low volume is generally unsustainable and often followed by a reversal. For this reason, E < R candles should be treated as warning signals that require caution.

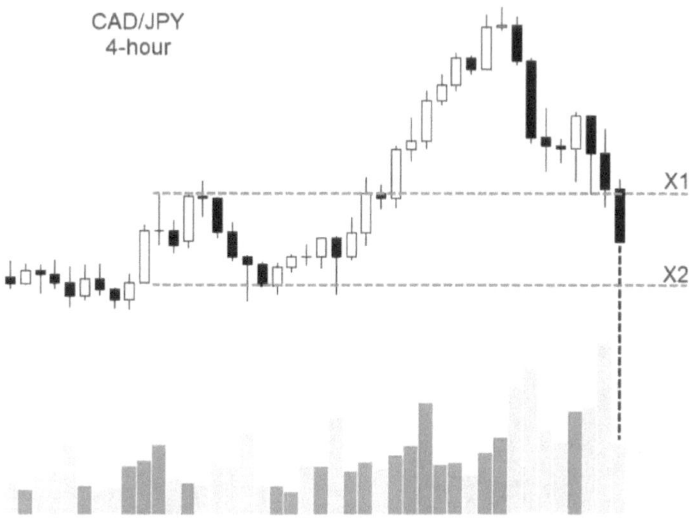

Figure 7.3: E<R - Example

Figure 7.3 illustrates the E < R candlestick pattern on the CAD/JPY 4-hour chart. The market is in an established uptrend, and the current phase represents a corrective pullback. Price has successfully broken above the swing high at X1, confirming that the bullish structure remains intact. A reasonable expectation is that price will pull back to test the support level at X2 before continuing higher.

During this corrective decline, a bearish candle appears with a notable characteristic. The candle has a solid body with minimal wicks—typically interpreted as strong and decisive selling. However, the volume of this candle is significantly lower than that of the previous candle, even though it produces a similar or larger price spread. This is a classic example of low effort producing a high result.

The contrast becomes even clearer when compared with the preceding candle, which shows an indecisive structure with upper and lower wicks but extremely high volume. Decisive price action on low volume following hesitation on high volume strongly suggests panic selling by retail traders rather than systematic distribution by smart money.

This combination of patterns within a corrective phase of an uptrend points to panic behavior rather than a genuine reversal. Retail traders are emotionally dumping positions without the participation of smart money, creating an unstable low that is vulnerable to reversal.

Although the pattern provides a strong preliminary signal, a prudent approach is to wait for a confirmation candle to verify that buying pressure is entering the market and that the reversal is indeed underway.

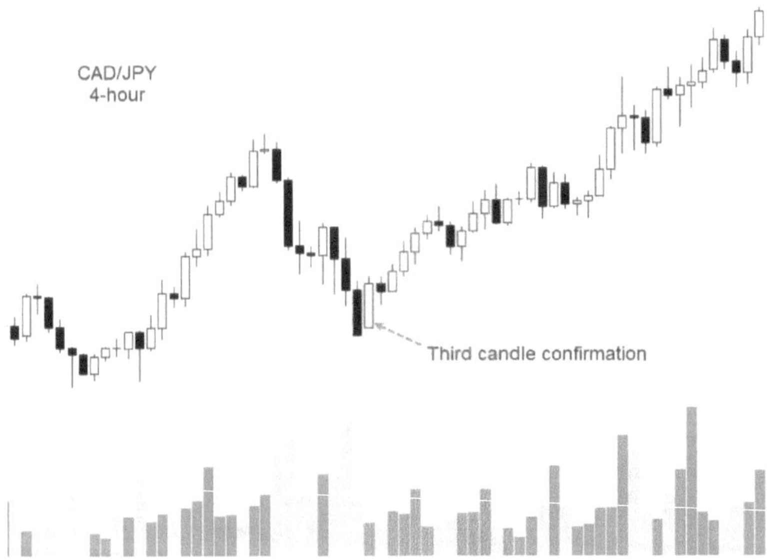

Figure 7.4: E<R - Example

Figure 7.4 shows the crucial role of the confirmation candle—the third candle—and the subsequent price development after it appears. This confirmation candle is a bullish candle with a large body that completely engulfs the body of the preceding bearish candle. It forms near the previous low and creates a strong reversal pattern. The move can also be interpreted as a false breakout of the prior low—price briefly breaks below the level and is quickly reclaimed.

If the panic-selling candle and this bullish confirmation candle are viewed together, the overall structure forms a clear rejection pattern with a long lower wick, reflecting strong buying rejection at the support zone. After the confirmation candle completes, price immediately rallies and breaks decisively above the prior high, continuing the original uptrend with clear momentum.

This sequence provides a textbook example of the combination: a bearish candle with effort smaller than result signaling panic selling, followed by a bullish confirmation candle with strong volume, creating a high-probability reversal setup.

E > R Pattern

Figure 7.5: Effort > Result

Figure 7.5 illustrates the second type of candle, characterized by the opposite condition—effort greater than result. This imbalance appears as high trading volume but a relatively small price spread, producing a narrow candle body despite strong market participation.

According to the Effort–Result Principle, a candle with such high volume—representing significant effort—would normally be expected to produce a correspondingly large bullish candle. That would be the result consistent with the level of effort invested.

But why does the candle here show only a narrow body? This suggests that substantial selling pressure exists in this price area, preventing price from rising strongly. No matter how large the upward effort may be, it produces only a small price result because it encounters resistance from sellers. This selling pressure may come from traders who previously bought at higher prices in this area and became trapped. When price returns to this zone, they seek to exit at breakeven, continuing to sell and thereby creating a steady supply.

In this scenario, one critical detail determines the market's next direction. If smart money is positioned as buyers, they must absorb this entire wave of selling pressure in order to push price higher toward their objective. Once the selling pressure has been fully absorbed and no more sellers remain willing to sell, even a small amount of additional demand can drive price sharply upward and break it out of the distribution zone, because the path has been cleared of obstacles. Conversely, if smart money is positioned as sellers, they have no incentive to absorb this supply. Instead, they will join the selling pressure and push the price downward. Determining which side smart money is on is the key to trading this candlestick scenario, and confirmation must come from the behavior of the next candle.

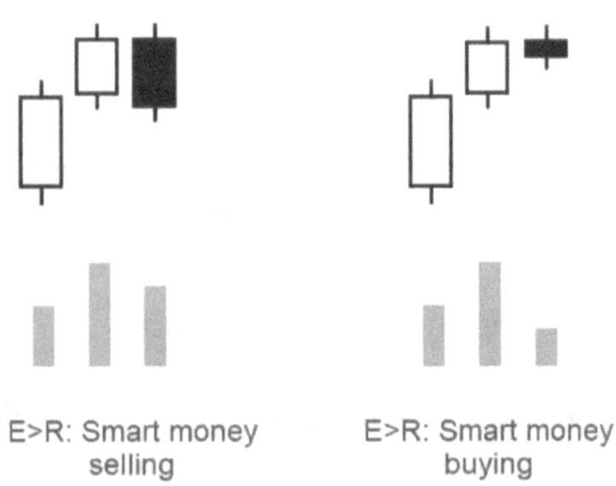

Figure 7.6: Smart money position revealed

Figure 7.6 illustrates the method of identifying smart money positioning through the third candle.

The illustration on the left shows smart money selling: after the second candle with high volume but narrow body, the third candle closes near the low of the second candle. This indicates that selling pressure is dominant and that smart money is distributing. The pattern serves as a warning of a potential bearish reversal.

The illustration on the right shows smart money buying: the third candle closes near the high of the second candle with declining volume, confirming that smart money has successfully absorbed the selling pressure and that the path has been cleared. This pattern signals bullish continuation.

The third confirmation candle plays a decisive role—it reveals where smart money is positioning and determines the appropriate trading direction.

Figure 7.7: E>R - Example

Figure 7.7 illustrates a case where an E > R candle appears. We observe a candle with a narrow spread despite having slightly higher volume than the preceding candle. The previous candle shows a long body with short wicks, indicating a strong bullish move, yet paradoxically it is accompanied by lower volume compared with the narrow-range candle under examination.

This imbalance—effort greater than result—suggests that significant selling pressure is absorbing the buying effort and preventing price from advancing strongly. To better understand the cause behind this phenomenon and confirm the positioning of smart money, we need to observe the next confirmation candle within the broader context of the overall market structure.

Before doing so, however, let us step back and examine the chart from a wider perspective to understand where this selling pressure may be emerging.

Figure 7.8: E>R - Example

Figure 7.8 provides the broader context that explains the cause behind the effort-greater-than-result pattern. The area marked by the dashed rectangle above highlights a significant resistance zone—where price previously began a sharp decline from a distribution phase. When price returns to this area after a long period of time, the psychology of traders who were trapped there becomes very clear.

These traders bought near the prior peak before the market collapsed and have been holding losing positions for an extended period. When price finally rallies back to their breakeven level, their natural reaction is to sell in order to exit the position and recover their capital rather than continue enduring uncertainty. This continuous selling pressure from trapped traders creates the situation where the upward effort—reflected by high volume—fails to produce a proportional result because price is constantly being suppressed.

No matter how much buying effort enters the market, it cannot drive price significantly higher when it encounters a wall of selling pressure from these trapped positions.

Figure 7.9: E>R - Example

Figure 7.9 demonstrates the decisive role of the third confirmation candle in determining the position of smart money. After the previous candle reveals an effort-greater-than-result condition, the key question becomes:

is smart money absorbing the selling orders from trapped traders in order to push price higher and break out of the distribution zone, or are they also positioned as sellers and prepared to sell alongside these trapped participants?

The third candle appears with a clear characteristic—it is a bearish candle whose open and close are both below the open of the previous narrow-body candle, and even below that candle's low. This pattern confirms that smart money is also positioning on the selling side and has no intention of absorbing the selling pressure in this area. Instead, they join the selling activity and push the market downward, as reflected in the subsequent price action when the market continues to decline sharply.

This bearish confirmation candle provides a clear sell signal. When large effort fails to produce a corresponding result and is followed by a decisive bearish candle, it serves as a strong warning of underlying weakness among buyers and the potential for a downward reversal.

Figure 7.10: E>R - Example

Figure 7.10 presents another case illustrating a similar pattern on the GBP/CHF pair on the daily timeframe. The area marked by the dashed rectangle above represents an important distribution zone where price previously consolidated for an extended period before collapsing sharply downward.

After the decline, price rallies back into this former distribution zone and forms a candle with a narrow body despite relatively high volume (the last candle shown in the figure), once again demonstrating the effort-greater-than-result pattern. Similar to the previous case, selling pressure from traders trapped in this zone prevents price from rising strongly despite the presence of significant buying effort.

The key question once again is whether smart money intends to absorb these selling orders in preparation for a new upward move, or whether they will join the selling pressure and push the market lower. To answer this question and determine the next direction, we must observe the third confirmation candle.

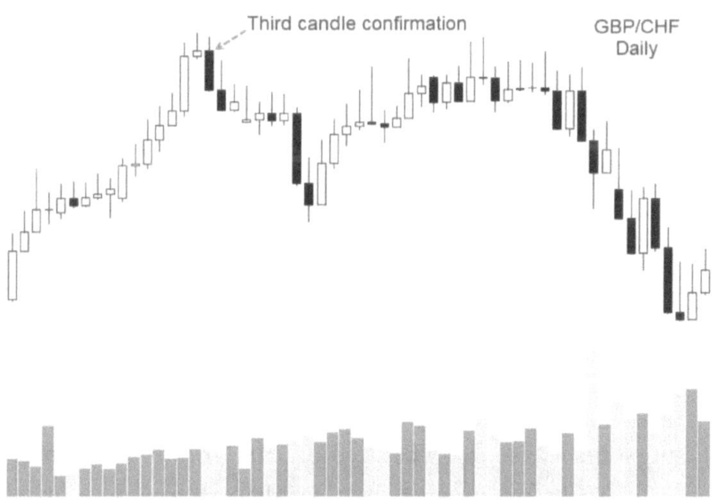

Figure 7.11: E>R - Example

Figure 7.11 shows the third confirmation candle appearing with a decisive characteristic. This candle is bearish, with its closing price clearly below the close of the previous narrow-body candle, confirming that smart money is also positioning on the selling side rather than absorbing the selling pressure.

This pattern indicates that they have no intention of defending this zone or preparing for a new upward move. Instead, they are actively participating in pushing the market lower.

The subsequent price action fully validates this assessment as the market continues to decline sharply with a sequence of consecutive bearish candles, demonstrating that selling pressure has taken complete control. The combination of identifying the effort-greater-than-result pattern at a resistance zone and receiving a bearish confirmation candle creates a high-probability short setup.

Figure 7.12: E>R - Example

Figure 7.12 presents a case from Bitcoin on the 1-hour timeframe, showing a variation of the effort-greater-than-result pattern. The marked area represents a distribution zone where price previously consolidated before sellers pushed the market downward in a strong decline. Buyers later attempt to push price back into this area.

Focus on the final candle in the figure. It is not an extremely narrow-body candle like the previous examples, but its spread is clearly smaller than that of the preceding candle despite having comparable volume. It therefore still falls into the effort-greater-than-result category, since the effort fails to produce a proportional expansion in price range.

The key question becomes whether smart money is positioned as buyers or sellers in this situation. To determine this, we must observe the third confirmation candle.

Figure 7.13: E>R - Example

Figure 7.13 shows the third confirmation candle appearing with a positive characteristic. This candle is bullish, with a closing price that exceeds the close of the previous candle and finishes near the high of that candle.

This pattern confirms that smart money is positioning on the buying side and has successfully absorbed the selling pressure from traders who were trapped in the previous distribution zone. With this absorption completed, the path is cleared for price to continue rallying and potentially break through the former distribution area. The subsequent price action fully confirms this assessment, as the market continues to rise strongly, eventually breaking successfully above the resistance zone and extending the upward trend.

Signals That Support/Resistance Is Likely to Hold

In this section, we examine how to identify when a resistance level is likely to hold and prevent price from breaking above it. As we know, breaking an important resistance level requires strong and sufficient buying demand to overcome all the selling pressure accumulated in that area.

Therefore, when observing price approaching a resistance level, if you notice that trading volume during the approach is progressively declining rather than increasing, this clearly indicates that there is not enough buying demand in that area to generate the momentum needed for a breakout. Declining volume as price approaches resistance is a clear signal of a lack of buyer participation, and as a result, the resistance level has a high probability of holding and pushing price back downward.

Figure 7.14: Resistance holds

Figure 7.14 illustrates a practical application on the EUR/USD 1-hour chart. The resistance level is tested twice, but with noticeably different volume characteristics.

During the first approach (the left area), price moves toward the resistance with relatively high volume, indicating that there is still significant buying effort. However, price fails to break through the level and is pushed back down, suggesting that the selling pressure at this resistance zone is stronger.

The key observation appears during the second approach (the right area). Volume declines significantly compared with the first test, indicating that buying demand is weakening and is no longer strong enough to challenge the resistance. With this declining volume, we can anticipate that the resistance level is likely to hold.

Subsequent price action confirms this expectation as bearish candles begin to appear with progressively increasing volume, showing that sellers have taken control and that price declines easily back toward the previous low.

Signals That a Support/Resistance Level Is Likely to Be Broken

Volume Signal

In this final section, we examine the opposite scenario—when a resistance level is likely to be broken. In contrast to the previous case, a resistance level tends to break when sufficient buying demand has accumulated and is strong enough to overcome the existing selling pressure.

Therefore, when we observe price approaching a resistance zone while trading volume progressively increases—rising with each rally—it clearly suggests that buying demand is being continuously injected into the market and that buyer participation is strengthening. This pattern of steadily increasing volume is a strong signal that the resistance level has a high probability of being broken on the next attempt.

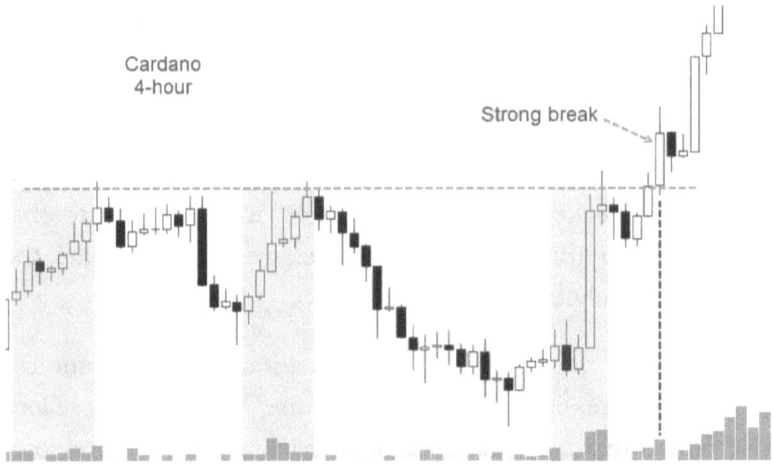

Figure 7.15: Resistance breaks

Figure 7.15 presents a real example on Cardano in the 4-hour timeframe, illustrating how buying demand gradually accumulates over three separate approaches to the resistance level, highlighted by the rectangular zones.

During the first approach (the left zone), buying volume is very low as price approaches resistance. Sellers easily cap the upward move and push price back down.

On the second approach (the middle zone), we can already see a noticeable increase in volume compared with the first attempt, indicating that stronger buying demand is being injected into the market. However, this volume is still not strong enough to push through the resistance level. Price then experiences a longer and deeper pullback than the previous one, suggesting that sellers still have enough strength to defend the resistance area.

By the third approach (the right zone), the volume mobilized by buyers increases even further compared with the second attempt, reflecting the growing determination of buyers to conquer this resistance level. A key difference appears when price encounters resistance this time. Although price is sold down, the decline occurs on very low volume, indicating that sellers no longer have the strength to defend the level as aggressively as before—they have become exhausted after the previous battles.

Moreover, this pullback lasts only three very short candles and is far shallower than the earlier ones. Shortly afterward, a strong breakout candle appears with volume significantly higher than the preceding bearish candles, clearly confirming that the resistance has been broken and that the balance of power has decisively shifted to the buyers. Price then continues to rally strongly following the breakout.

Candlestick Pattern Signal

There is another situation in which we can anticipate that a resistance level is likely to be broken—when price forms a sideways consolidation right below the resistance instead of being pushed down sharply.

The logic behind this pattern is quite straightforward. Under normal circumstances, when price approaches a key resistance level, selling pressure at that area should be strong enough to push price decisively lower, creating a clear rejection. However, if price is not strongly rejected and instead forms a sideways base—moving back and forth within a narrow range just beneath the resistance—it sends an important message: sellers no longer have enough strength to push price into a deep decline as they did during previous tests.

At the same time, the formation of this sideways base suggests that buyers are gradually overwhelming the sellers. They are absorbing the available selling pressure without allowing price to fall far, while quietly accumulating positions in preparation for the next breakout attempt.

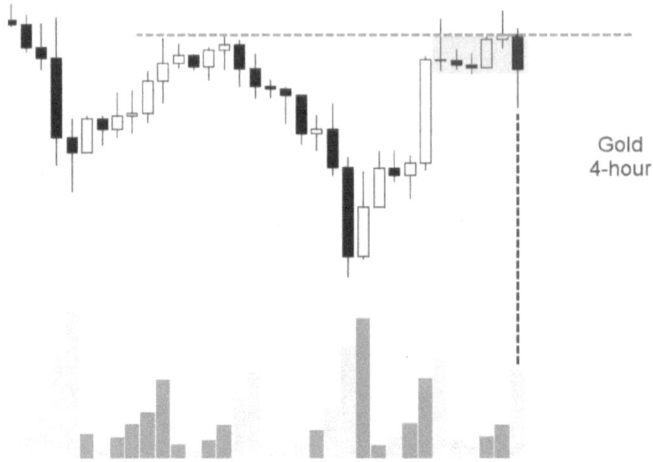

Figure 7.16: Resistance breaks

Figure 7.16 shows an example on the 4-hour gold chart. As price approaches the resistance level, instead of being strongly rejected, it forms a sideways consolidation zone highlighted by the rectangular box—this is the first signal of weakening sellers. The most important detail appears in the final candle within this zone. If you are familiar with the concept of greater effort versus weaker result, you will immediately recognize this as a classic example of that pattern. It is a bearish candle with a very long lower wick despite strong selling volume.

The logic behind this candle is straightforward. When price approaches resistance, selling pressure is naturally expected, and the high volume reflects that strong selling activity. However, this selling effort fails to produce the expected result. If sellers were truly in control and pushing price down decisively, the candle should close with a full bearish body and little or no lower wick. Instead, the candle leaves a long lower wick, showing that although sellers tried to push price lower with significant volume, buyers quickly stepped in and absorbed the selling pressure.

That long lower wick is therefore clear evidence that sellers no longer have the strength to drive price into a deeper decline. Buyers are able to absorb the heavy selling without allowing price to move far away from the resistance level, and they even manage to push price back upward. This is a strong confirmation that the balance of power is shifting toward the buyers and that the market is preparing for a potential breakout.

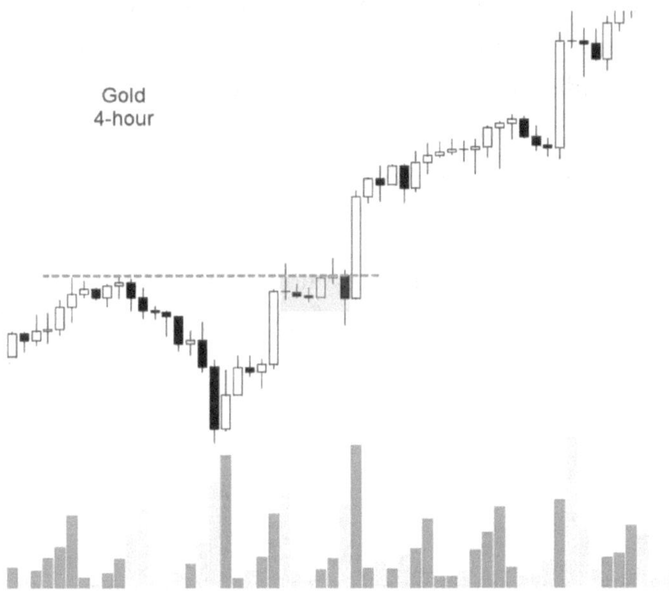

Figure 7.17: Resistance breaks

Figure 7.17 shows what happens immediately afterward. Price quickly breaks out of the sideways consolidation and rallies strongly above the resistance level, forming a sequence of bullish candles with clear momentum. This rally is both powerful and sustained, confirming that the combination of the rejection candle—an example of greater effort with weaker result—together with the sideways accumulation zone has created an exceptionally strong breakout setup.

With that, we have reached the end of Chapter 7. In this chapter, the discussion shifts from theory to tactical execution—where volume and candlestick structure combine to produce actionable signals. Patterns such as smaller effort than result and greater effort than result become lenses through which we decode the meaning behind each candle, allowing us to go beyond simply observing what happened and begin to understand why it happened and what may come next.

Candles showing smaller effort than result often reveal panic and FOMO—typical retail behaviors that lack smart money backing and are therefore vulnerable to reversals. In contrast, candles showing greater effort than result highlight absorption battles: situations where trapped sellers create supply or where smart money quietly accumulates positions, with the third candle often revealing the market's true direction. Declining volume as price approaches resistance warns of insufficient demand to break the level, while increasing volume or sideways consolidation signals accumulation that may precede a breakout.

By this point, we have covered nearly all the core skills needed to prepare for a complete trading strategy. In the next chapter, we will walk through the full process of preparing for trade entries and managing positions in a structured and practical way.

CHAPTER 8: THE SMT FRAMEWORK

Across the previous seven chapters, we have built a complete analytical toolkit. In this chapter, we will bring all those elements together into a systematic process—from identifying trading zones and evaluating momentum to pinpointing precise entry points, setting logical stop-loss levels, and managing positions through to profit-taking. Many traders possess excellent analytical skills but still struggle with execution because they lack a clear process. They can identify market structure and sense opportunities, yet they often hesitate when it comes to triggering an entry, placing a stop, or managing the trade once it is open.

In Chapter 8, we introduce the SMT system (Structure, Momentum, Trigger)—a three-step framework you will apply to execute trades. These three steps are not independent but interconnected, with each step building on the previous one to create high-probability trading decisions. We will break down each step with detailed guidance, clear criteria, and practical applications so that you can execute trades with confidence and consistency.

Overview of the SMT System

The SMT system is a three-step sequential process that helps traders move from simply observing the market to executing actionable trades. The first step is Structure—identifying the market structure so we understand where the market currently stands and which direction is worth trading. The second step is Momentum—evaluating the strength of the move to determine whether the trend has enough energy to continue. The third step is Trigger—waiting for a confirmation signal before executing the trade, with a clearly defined entry point, a logical stop-loss, and a reasonable profit target.

These three steps must be followed in order. Momentum cannot be evaluated properly without first understanding the market structure, and a valid trigger cannot be recognized without the context provided by momentum. This sequential process ensures that every trading decision is based on a complete understanding of the market rather than on isolated observations.

More importantly, the SMT system does not only tell you when to enter a trade—it also tells you, just as importantly, when not to trade. In many cases, after completing all three steps of analysis, the correct decision is to stay out of the market because the conditions are not yet favorable. This discipline is what separates consistent traders from gamblers.

Step 1: Structure Analysis

The first step in any trading analysis is to identify the market structure. Structure provides the context—it tells you the direction of the trend, highlights the key levels, and establishes the overall bias for trading decisions. Without a clear understanding of structure, momentum signals and entry triggers become ambiguous and far less reliable.

Objective

The objective of this step is to answer three fundamental questions:

1. What type of market condition are we dealing with—is the market in an uptrend, a downtrend, or moving sideways?
2. Where are the key support and resistance areas, and which zones deserve the most attention?
3. What should your trading bias be—should you prioritize long trades, favor short positions, or remain neutral for the time being?

Process for Identifying Market Structure

Identify Swing Highs and Swing Lows

We begin by marking the swing highs and swing lows on the chart using the principles introduced in Chapter 2. These are the building blocks of structure analysis. In practical trading, we usually focus on advanced swing highs and swing lows—the swings that truly matter within the broader trend structure.

Determine the Trend Direction

Once the swings have been identified, apply the rules that define market trends:

An uptrend is confirmed when:

- Swing highs are consistently broken, meaning price forms higher highs
- Swing lows remain intact, meaning price maintains higher lows

A downtrend is confirmed when:

- Swing lows are consistently broken, meaning price forms lower lows
- Swing highs remain intact, meaning price maintains lower highs

A sideways market occurs when:

- Both swing highs and swing lows are broken inconsistently, or
- Neither side is clearly broken, and price remains confined within a range

Mark Key Support and Resistance Zones

After identifying the trend, the next step is to mark the important zones based on the major swing levels.

Support zones are drawn from structural/major swing lows. These areas act as the "home base of buyers"—zones where buying interest has historically stepped in with strength.

Resistance zones are drawn from structural/major swing highs. These represent the "stronghold of the bears"—areas where sellers have historically defended the market.

Reversal zones should also be kept in mind. When a resistance level is broken, it often turns into support, and the opposite is also true: once support is broken, it can later act as resistance.

Narrow the Trading Zone

Once the key levels have been identified, you can define the "trading zone"—the area between the nearest support and resistance where the current price action is taking place. This becomes the primary focus for the next stage of momentum analysis.

Narrowing the trading zone helps in several ways:

- It focuses your attention on the most relevant price action
- It reduces noise from less important areas of the chart
- It establishes clear boundaries for your trading plan

If you cannot answer these points clearly, do not move on to Step 2. Go back to the chart, review the swing structure, and clarify the market structure first. Trading without structural clarity is gambling, not trading.

Step 2: Momentum Evaluation

Once the market structure is clear, the second step is to evaluate momentum—assessing whether the trend still has enough strength to continue or is beginning to show signs of exhaustion. Momentum analysis answers a key question: is this a favorable moment to trade in the direction of the trend bias?

Objective

This step focuses on identifying three key aspects:

- Is the trend strengthening or weakening?
- Are there signs of trend continuation or a potential reversal?
- How is smart money positioning in the market?

Momentum assessment is not based on a single indicator but on the convergence of multiple factors. We evaluate momentum through several key dimensions, as outlined below.

Methods for Assessing Momentum

- Comparing the volume of two waves moving in the same direction
- Comparing the volume of two waves moving in opposite directions
- Comparing impulse wave progression
- Comparing the depth of pullback waves
- Comparing the angle of impulse waves and pullbacks

- Comparing the slope within individual waves
- Identifying wave-volume and candle–volume imbalances (E>R and E<R)

Note: Not all seven methods need to align perfectly. However, the more factors that converge, the stronger the trading setup becomes.

Part 3: Trade Trigger

With the market structure clearly defined and momentum assessed as favorable, the final step is to wait for a trigger signal before executing the trade. This is the point where analysis turns into action—where you actually press the buy or sell button.

Objective

This step provides:

- A precise entry point at a specific price level
- A logical stop-loss placement based on market structure
- A reasonable profit target with a favorable risk–reward ratio

A trigger is not about guessing the timing of the market. Instead, it is a systematic confirmation that waits for specific price action signals before entering the trade.

Trigger Signals

The core trigger signal in the SMT system is the "confirmation candle." This candle confirms that the opposing side has lost control and is no longer able to resist effectively, allowing the dominant side to initiate a buy or sell position at the close of that candle. So, what types of candles can serve as this confirmation signal?

Trigger Signal 1: The Third Candle After an E>R Pattern

The E>R pattern is a common formation that often signals the exhaustion of either an impulse wave or a corrective wave. This creates an ideal context for waiting for the appearance of the third candle. After the E>R candle forms, we still cannot immediately conclude where smart money is positioned. One more candle is needed for confirmation.

The pattern typically unfolds as follows:

- The first candle: Establishes the context
- The second candle: The E>R signal (high volume, narrow spread, with a rejection wick)
- The third candle: Confirmation (a close near the high or the low of the second candle reveals the side favored by smart money)

Bullish Confirmation Pattern

For long trades, the confirmation candle should close near the high of the preceding E>R candle, or even better, close entirely above the E>R candle.

Typical characteristics include:

- A larger candle body, reflecting stronger conviction
- Potentially accompanied by increasing volume
- Clear rejection of lower price levels

Bearish Confirmation Pattern

For short trades, the pattern works in the opposite way. The confirmation candle should close near the low of the preceding E>R candle, or close entirely below the E>R candle.

Trigger Signal 2: Testing

I devoted an entire chapter to the concept of Testing and its role in confirming the exhaustion of one side before we enter a trade in the opposite direction. In reality, the E>R pattern does not always appear, and in those situations, testing becomes a powerful tool for evaluating market momentum. It acts like a clearing process—removing the remaining pockets of uncertainty and paving the way for a more confident trade entry.

In most cases, traders can enter a position once the testing phase has been completed.

Trade Execution

Entry Point

The entry should never be vague—never something like "enter somewhere around here." It must be clearly defined:

- Trigger Signal 1: Entry = the closing price of the confirmation candle

- Trigger Signal 2: Entry = the closing price of the final testing candle

A clearly defined entry price allows you to determine the correct position size and removes emotional decision-making during live trading.

Stop-Loss Placement

The stop-loss should be placed beyond the invalidation point—the level where, if price reaches it, the trade setup is clearly proven wrong.

For long trades:

- Below the rejection wick of the E>R candle
- Below the structural swing low (if the wick is not excessively deep)

If the wick is extremely long, placing the stop directly below it may result in a poor risk–reward ratio. In such cases, the trader should wait for additional price action to find a more reasonable entry with a tighter stop-loss—for example, waiting for the market to perform a low-volume testing phase before entering.

For short trades:

- Above the rejection wick of the E>R candle
- Above the structural swing high

Stop-Loss Size Considerations

As a general guideline, risking around 1–2% of the trading account per stop-loss is considered reasonable.

Profit Targets

The SMT system suggests two primary approaches to taking profits:

Approach 1: Fixed Risk–Reward Ratio

Target = 2R (twice the distance from entry to stop-loss) — highly recommended. Of course, a 3R target would be even better, but through experience and practice, I personally prefer setting the target at 2R when a clear support or resistance level is not available for targeting. A minimum risk–reward ratio of 1:2 means you only need a win rate above 33% to remain profitable over time.

Advantages:

- Consistent and rule-based
- Does not rely on subjective level identification
- Automatically ensures a positive risk–reward ratio

Disadvantages:

- May miss larger moves if the trend continues strongly
- The exit may occur before price actually reaches a major resistance level

Approach 2: The Nearest Key Level

Target = the nearest key resistance (for long trades) or the nearest key support (for short trades). This approach is structure-based, aiming to exit the trade at levels where the opposing side is likely to become active.

Advantages:

- Aligned with the actual structure of the market

- Helps avoid getting caught in reversals at important levels

Disadvantages:

- The key level may be very close (resulting in a poor risk–reward ratio) or very far away (making the target unrealistic)
- Requires some subjective judgment when determining which levels are truly "important"

Approach 3: The Hybrid Approach

This method combines the two approaches by using partial profit-taking.

Step 1: When price reaches 2R, close 50% of the position and move the stop-loss to the entry price (breakeven).

Step 2: Let the remaining 50% run toward the nearest key resistance or support level.

This approach:

- Locks in profits early, reducing psychological pressure
- Still allows you to capture extended moves if the trend continues
- Protects the trade against reversals by using a breakeven stop
- Works well across different market conditions while maintaining trading discipline.

Trade Management After Entry

Once a trade has been entered with the stop-loss and target already defined, trade management involves the following principles:

- Monitor Without Over-Managing: Trust your analysis and allow the trade to develop. Constant interference usually causes more harm than good.

- Move the Stop to Breakeven When Appropriate: Once the trade moves favorably, consider shifting the stop-loss to the entry price. This removes the risk of loss while still allowing the trade to continue toward its profit potential.

- Watch for Changes in Momentum: If price is approaching the target but momentum suddenly shifts—for example, strong rejection candles appear on high volume—consider exiting early even before the target is reached. However, do not exit simply because price pauses or consolidates briefly. Healthy trends often include pullbacks. Only exit if clear reversal signals appear.

- Trailing Stops for Extended Moves: If price continues strongly beyond the initial target and momentum remains solid, a trailing stop strategy may be used—gradually moving the stop higher to lock in additional profit while allowing the trend to continue. However, trailing stops require experience. Beginners are better off following fixed targets first in order to build consistency.

When Not to Take a Trade

Knowing when not to trade is just as important as knowing when to enter. The ability to step aside acts as a long-term shield that protects traders from unnecessary losses.

We stay out of the market when:

- The structure is unclear — it is not obvious whether the market is in an uptrend or a downtrend.

- Momentum signals are mixed — some factors are bullish while others are bearish, with no clear overall picture.
- There is no confirmation candle — impatience leads to entering too early without waiting for the third candle.
- The stop-loss is too wide — the setup requires an unreasonably large stop relative to the potential reward.
- The target is too close — the nearest support or resistance is so close that a 2R target cannot be achieved.
- Your emotional state is unstable — trading while angry, desperate, or overly confident often leads to mistakes.

Better trades will always come. The discipline to wait for the right setups is what separates consistent winners from everyone else.

We have now walked through the complete three-step process for executing trades with confidence and discipline. There were many bullet points, many guidelines, and many reminders along the way—all designed to help you achieve the best possible trading positions. You may already have a general picture forming in your mind, but it is probably not yet a fully concrete one. That is completely normal. Trade execution is one of the most skill-intensive parts of trading. It is practical and experiential rather than purely theoretical. It can be challenging, but that challenge is exactly what helps the lessons stay with you and eventually become second nature.

Everything you have just read should serve as a practical handbook—something you will want to keep close, or ideally commit to memory over time. Of course, that only happens once these skills become familiar through repeated practice. To make the ideas in this chapter clearer and more tangible, I have also prepared visual presentations of the key strategies discussed above.

In the next chapter, things become even more exciting. You will see these principles applied in real-world trading situations through actual trade examples. Let's move on to Chapter 9.

CHAPTER 9: REAL-WORLD TRADE EXAMPLES

In the previous chapter, I walked you through the detailed process of entering and managing trades. The SMT system is not only a framework for evaluating and applying momentum trading; it is also a toolkit for mastering market reading. In other words, even if you follow a different trading methodology, you can still apply parts of this framework to enhance your market analysis. That is why I believe the momentum system presented in this book can be useful for virtually all traders.

Although I have tried to present the strategy carefully and in detail, I never conclude my books without providing concrete real-world examples to illustrate the concepts. In this chapter, I will walk you through six different trades across multiple asset classes, including stocks, commodities, forex, and cryptocurrencies. I intentionally diversified the markets in these examples because the SMT system can be applied across all financial markets.

Now, let's begin with the first trade example.

Trade Example 1

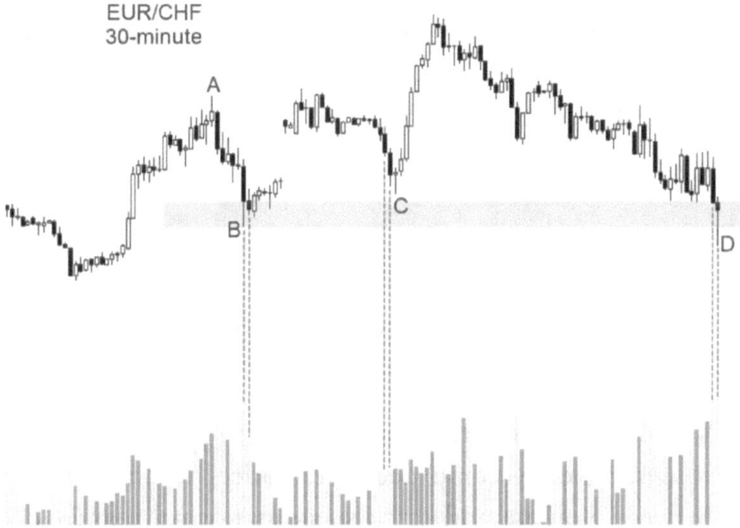

Figure 9.1: Example 1

We begin with the Forex market, looking at the EUR/CHF pair on the 30-minute timeframe.

Step 1: Identify the market structure

The analysis shows that the pair is in a clear uptrend. Swing high A has been broken, while swing low B remains intact and has not been violated. Since the structure is bullish, our bias is to look for a buy opportunity.

Now let's examine the swing low in this case more carefully. Why is it B and not C? Both B and C qualify as swing lows under the basic five-candle rule. However, identifying an advanced swing low requires additional criteria. In this situation, B represents the deeper low within the market's pullback, which makes it the advanced swing low according to the criteria established in Chapter 2.

Correctly identifying the swing low is extremely important. If you mistakenly choose C, then the current price action would appear to have already broken the swing low, which could make you uncertain about whether to prepare for a buy or a sell. But once the correct swing low is identified at B, the context becomes clear: price is pulling back toward the buyers' stronghold—the support area at B.

Step 2: Evaluate Momentum

The market is clearly going through a series of pullbacks, so let's examine what these pullbacks reveal about momentum.

At low B: Volume and price are consistent. When volume increases, price declines strongly; when volume decreases, price declines weakly. This alignment between volume and price suggests normal market behavior, with no clear buying or selling signal yet.

At low C: The volume of the second candle is slightly higher than that of the previous one. However, the bodies of the two candles are roughly similar in size, while the second candle has a longer wick. This may be the first sign of volume–spread asymmetry. As you can see, price reverses upward afterward. However, this is still not an ideal entry point because the reward–risk ratio is not particularly attractive—the nearest resistance is relatively close to the potential entry.

At low D: This is where the market experiences the strongest pullback. Traders who do not study momentum might become nervous when they see such a deep correction, but momentum analysis actually provides strong confidence in this situation for two reasons.

First, the slope of the correction wave: In this third pullback, the slope is noticeably flatter compared to the previous two pullbacks. This indicates that the selling pressure is weakening.

Second, the volume–spread relationship in the final two candles at low D: There is a clear asymmetry. An E>R candle appears—its volume is roughly equal to the previous candle, but instead of forming a large-bodied candle with short wicks, it appears as a pin bar. This is a very clear rejection of selling pressure by the buyers.

Even so, we still cannot conclude that price will reverse immediately. At this stage, we wait for the next candle—the third candle—to confirm whether smart money is truly aligning with the buyers.

Step 3: Trade Trigger

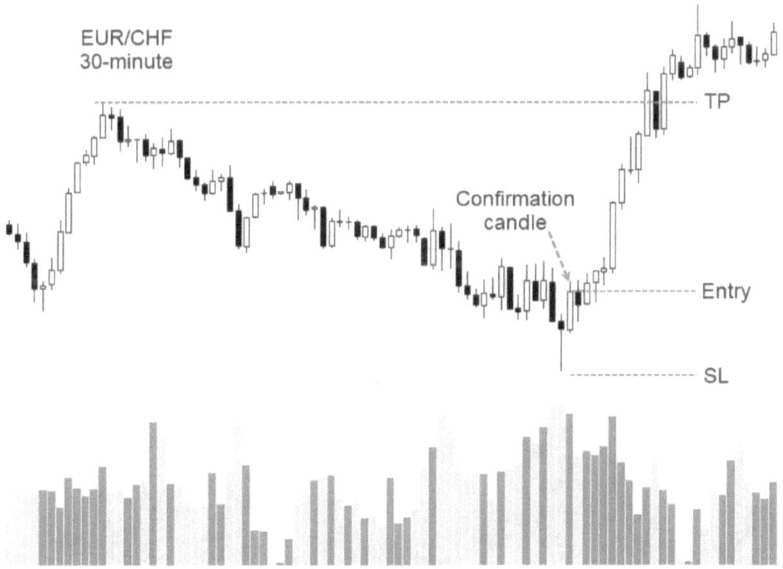

Figure 9.2: Example 2

Figure 9.2 gives us a clear confirmation candle—a long-bodied bullish candle that closes completely above the previous pin bar. The intention of smart money has clearly aligned with the buyers, reflected in both the high volume and the strong bullish spread. At this point, the situation is clear, and we can set up a buy trade according to the system.

Entry: At the close of the confirmation candle.

Stop-loss: Since the rejection wick of the pin bar is not excessively long, the stop-loss can be placed just below the wick without negatively affecting the risk–reward ratio.

Take-profit: We can see that the nearest resistance level roughly aligns with the 2R level (twice the distance from entry to stop-loss). That provides a reasonable target for this trade. As shown in Figure 9.2, price moves smoothly to reach our intended take-profit level.

This first real-world example establishes the foundation for a systematic analytical process. The three steps—Structure, Momentum, and Trigger—are applied consistently to identify high-probability trading opportunities. The following examples will continue to demonstrate this framework across different market conditions and asset classes, helping you develop stronger pattern recognition and greater trading confidence.

Trade Example 2

Figure 9.3: Example 2

Next, we move to the crypto market, looking at the Bitcoin price chart on the Daily timeframe. Let's continue sharpening the three-step analysis process with this example.

Step 1: Identify the Market Structure

The Bitcoin chart can be divided into two halves: the left side and the right side.

On the left side of the chart, we can clearly see that swing highs are being broken, while no swing lows are being broken to the downside. In contrast, on the right side, the bears consistently break through swing lows while swing highs remain intact. This shows a clear transition of the market from an uptrend to a downtrend.

Next, we identify the key zones on the chart using the swing highs and swing lows.

On the left side, the key support zone lies around swing low A. This is a valid advanced swing low according to the principles introduced earlier in the book. But why is it A rather than C or D?

D cannot be considered a swing low in this case because the price movement from D did not break the nearest previous high in a valid way. As for C, the price from C did break the previous high at B, satisfying a criterion that D does not meet. However, if we examine point B more closely, it corresponds to a bearish candle with both a long body and long wicks, spanning across many candles on both its left and right sides. Even if we extend that candle, B still does not qualify as a swing high under the five-candle rule.

Because of this relationship between swing highs and swing lows, C cannot be considered a valid basic swing low, let alone an advanced one. Therefore, the support zone should be drawn from the low at A, which belongs to the earlier bullish structure.

On the right side of the chart, both E and F meet the criteria to be considered advanced swing highs. However, F has just been broken by the buyers, as shown by the final two candles in Figure 9.3 closing completely above that swing high. As a result, our focus now shifts to the resistance zone at swing high E.

By identifying the support and resistance zones, we have effectively narrowed down the trading zone, which now lies between the two rectangles marked on the chart. At this point, let's zoom into the chart and move on to evaluating momentum.

Step 2: Evaluate Momentum

Figure 9.4: Example 2

First, notice the corrective wave from X to Y. It is flatter than the previous pullback waves, isn't it? This suggests that the buyers' momentum in pushing the price upward has already begun to weaken. Of course, we cannot draw a firm conclusion yet, but it is the first signal worth paying attention to.

Next, look at the last two candles on the chart and their corresponding volume. The second candle clearly has higher volume than the previous one, yet the result is a candle with a small body and an upper wick. This is a classic E>R candle—greater effort but smaller result, showing a clear imbalance.

The reason for this imbalance is quite understandable, because price is approaching the bears' stronghold above. As price moves closer to the resistance zone, selling pressure naturally increases, resulting in a candle with such a limited spread. At this stage, we wait for the confirmation candle to determine which side smart money is actually supporting.

Step 3: Trade Trigger

Figure 9.5: Example 2

The confirmation candle once again appears as a small-bodied candle with a long upper wick, closing near the close of the previous candle—a signal that smart money is siding with the sellers. If you still feel uncertain because the candle is technically bullish, you may wait for the next two candles to obtain stronger confirmation.

The entry, stop-loss, and take-profit levels are illustrated in Figure 9.5. Whether you choose a take-profit at 2R (twice the distance from entry to stop-loss) or at the nearest support level, the target is achieved in this trade. This example clearly shows how correctly identifying market structure and the key support/resistance zones creates a strong foundation for analyzing momentum and finding a precise entry point.

Trade Example 3

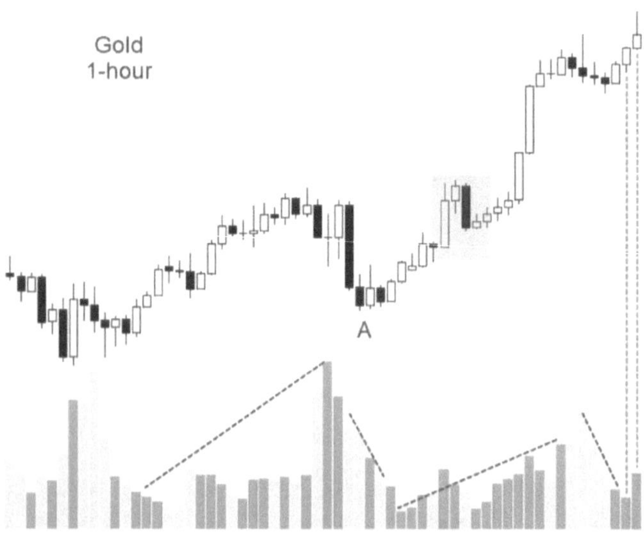

Figure 9.6: Example 3

Next, we move to an example from the precious metals market. Figure 9.6 presents the gold price on the 1-hour timeframe. Let's see what analytical insights this chart provides.

Step 1: Identify the Market Structure

On the chart, we can see that gold has broken through several swing highs, while no swing lows have been broken to the downside. This indicates a clear uptrend, meaning we should prioritize buy setups rather than sell opportunities. The structural swing low lies at point A. This is the lowest point from which price subsequently broke the previous swing high.

I have also drawn a rectangle box on the chart. It is important to note that within this cluster of candles, there are actually no valid swing highs or swing lows. The reason is that this group of candles does not form a swing low that satisfies the five-candle rule. Therefore, when considering the relationship between swing lows and swing highs, we cannot classify any point within this cluster as a valid swing.

Step 2: Evaluate Momentum

We evaluate the market's momentum across two dimensions.

First, the volume of the bullish waves versus the bearish waves. On the chart, the two bullish waves show increasing volume, while the two bearish waves show decreasing volume. According to the rule of comparing the volume of opposing waves, rising volume during bullish waves combined with declining volume during bearish waves suggests that the market still has potential to move higher. In this case, bullish momentum is strengthening.

Next, we examine the relationship between candlesticks and volume. Once again, our attention goes to the final two candles on the chart. We see another E>R candle. The second candle has significantly higher volume than the first one, yet its body is only similar in size to the previous candle and it even has a long upper wick. This result is not proportional to the effort reflected in the candle's volume. Selling pressure around this resistance zone prevents price from extending upward despite the strong buying effort.

When price approaches a resistance area, bears tend to step in and sell. This selling pressure means that even strong buying effort may fail to push the price higher. If smart money is truly aligned with the buyers, they must absorb that selling pressure. Only after absorbing those sell orders can price rally higher. Therefore, we wait for the third candle to appear in order to evaluate whether smart money is genuinely supporting the buyers.

Step 3: Trade Trigger

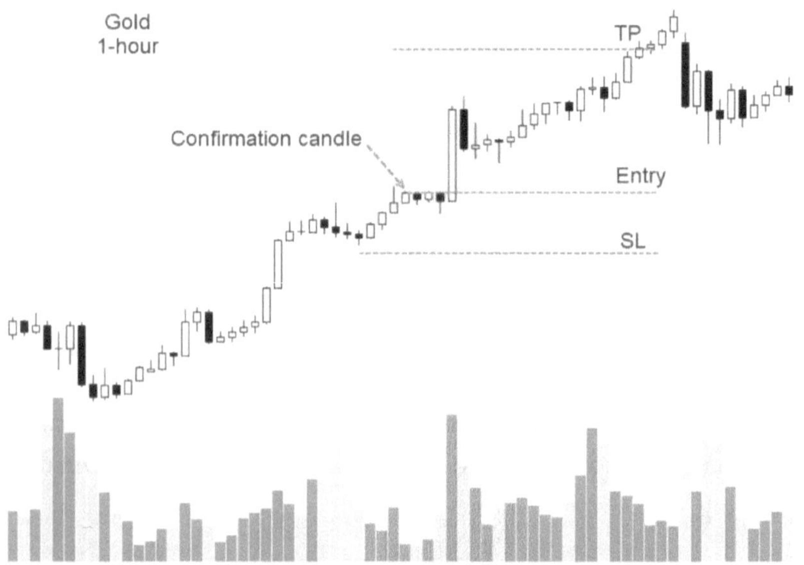

Figure 9.7: Example 3

The confirmation candle closes near the high of the previous candle. This pattern indicates that smart money is siding with the buyers. Another point to notice is the behavior of the candles that follow the confirmation candle, along with their volume. If smart money were selling, the volume should be high and accompanied by bearish candles with sufficiently large bodies—not small-bodied bearish candles like those shown in Figure 9.7.

The entry, stop-loss, and take-profit levels are illustrated on the chart. With a take-profit target set at 2R, the trade reaches its objective without much difficulty.

Trade Example 4

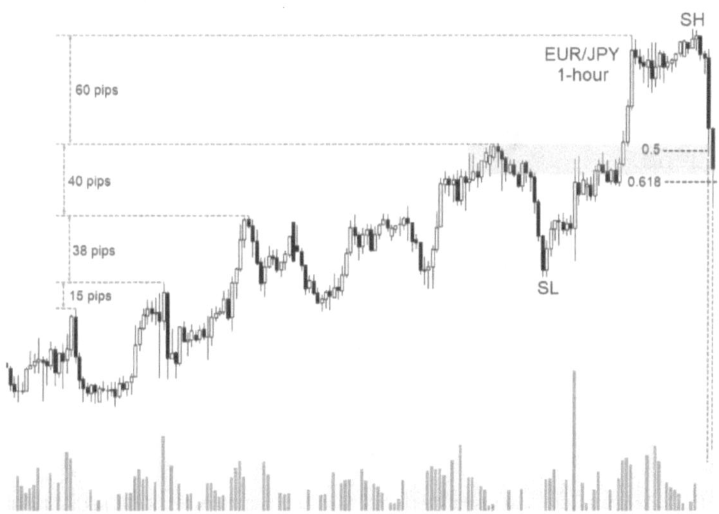

Figure 9.8: Example 4

Next, we move to another currency pair: EUR/JPY on the 1-hour timeframe. We will continue using the familiar formula: Market Structure + Momentum + Trigger.

Step 1: Identify the Market Structure

The EUR/JPY chart shows that swing highs are being broken consistently, while swing lows remain intact. This clearly indicates that the pair is experiencing a strong uptrend. I have also marked the nearest swing high and swing low relative to the current price level on the chart. These levels form the zone where we will look for additional signals from the market. We will examine this area more closely in the next step.

Step 2: Evaluate Momentum

First, let's look at the expansion of the impulse waves. As marked in Figure 9.8, the increase in impulse wave size is very clear: from 15 pips to 38 pips, then 40 pips, and finally 60 pips. The spacing between impulse waves keeps increasing. This pattern shows that buyers are pushing price further with each wave. It is a very positive supporting factor for trend continuation. Increasing impulse spacing signals accelerating momentum and a strong underlying trend.

Next, when price pulls back, it is supported by a zone marked with a rectangle on the chart. This area was originally a resistance zone drawn from a previous swing high, but once it was broken, it naturally transformed into a support zone. This provides another piece of evidence supporting a bullish bias at this stage.

Furthermore, when we apply the Fibonacci retracement tool from the swing high to the swing low marked on the chart, price is currently aligning with the 0.5 to 0.618 Fibonacci retracement levels. This confluence further confirms that the area acts as a strong demand zone.

Note: This detail goes beyond the core momentum concepts discussed in this book, but it is a very valuable additional factor that increases confidence in the bullish bias in this situation. If you want to explore Fibonacci levels in more depth, I highly recommend my bestseller Secrets on Fibonacci Trading. You can find it on the last page of this book, along with access to my full book portfolio.

Most importantly, when price pulls back into this demand zone, we can clearly observe an Effort–Result discrepancy between the last two candles on the chart, both of which are bearish. Specifically, the second candle shows higher volume than the previous one, yet it has a noticeably smaller body and a long lower wick. This demonstrates a clear imbalance between volume and spread, forming an E>R candle according to the concept we studied earlier.

What does this E>R candle tell us? It indicates that strong buyers are present in this area. As analyzed earlier, this is a powerful demand zone because it represents both a support area and a Fibonacci confluence. The analysis suggests that buyers are actively waiting here. As soon as price declines into this zone, they step in quickly and aggressively to buy. As a result, the selling effort is absorbed by the buyers. Despite significant selling pressure, price fails to decline deeply. An E>R pattern with high selling volume but minimal price decline signals strong buying absorption.

Step 3: Trade Trigger

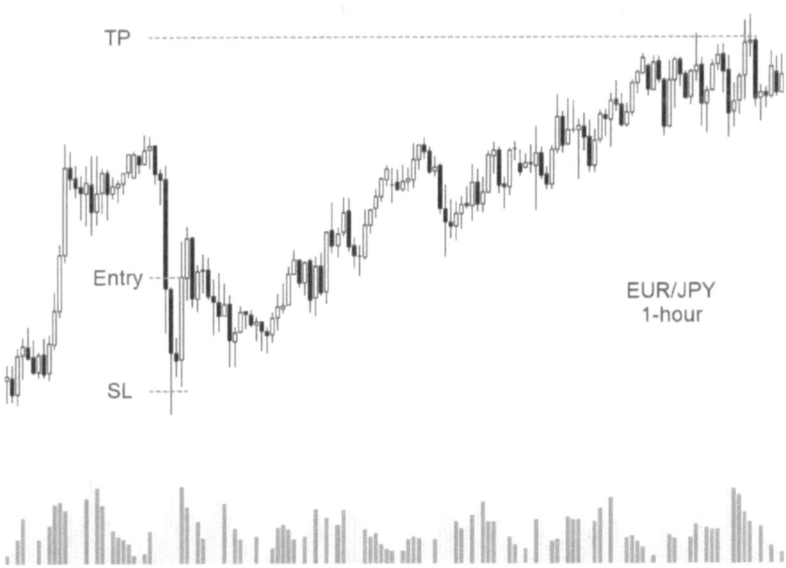

Figure 9.9: Example 4

We wait for a signal that buyers are participating. The third candle—the confirmation candle—appears as a very small-bodied candle completely contained within the previous candle. However, the candle that follows reveals the true strength of the buyers: a strong bullish candle with a very large body and rising volume, engulfing the two preceding bearish candles. At this point, the buy trade is triggered. The entry, stop-loss, and take-profit levels are illustrated on the chart. A profit target at 2R allows the trade to lock in a solid gain.

Observing the chart, you can see that on the way toward the take-profit target, price experiences some hesitation near the most recent swing high. This is exactly why I often prefer taking profits near the nearest key zone. Nevertheless, in this example we have many factors supporting the bullish bias, so it is reasonable to expect price to extend beyond the previous high—at least until we begin to see signs that impulse waves are no longer expanding.

If you are a more conservative trader, you may choose to lock in profits once price reaches the nearest key resistance, move the stop-loss to the entry level, and allow half of the remaining position to continue running toward the 2R target.

Trade Example 5

Figure 9.10: Example 5

Next, we move to another cryptocurrency example—NEAR—and explore how the art of entering a trade using testing can provide an advantage for our trading decisions.

Step 1: Identify the Market Structure

Figure 9.10 presents the NEAR price chart on the Daily timeframe. It is easy to confirm that NEAR is in an uptrend. Even though I have not marked every swing high and swing low on the chart, it is clear that price repeatedly breaks through swing highs while no swing lows are subsequently broken to the downside. In a chart like this, we naturally prioritize buy opportunities and focus on identifying potential swing low areas where an entry might occur.

I have marked six swing highs and swing lows on the chart—A, B, C, D, E, and F. Which one is the swing low in this case? The answer is B. It represents the lowest point of the pullback from A, and from B, price clearly breaks above the previous swing high at A.

If you think D is the swing low, that would be a mistake. The reason is simple: price from D has not broken above the preceding swing high at C. In other words, the market has not formed a candle that closes completely above swing high C, including both its body and wick. Therefore, D cannot be considered an advanced swing low in this case.

Step 2: Evaluate Momentum

I have drawn a support zone on the chart. It is derived from swing high A. Initially, this level acted as resistance, but once it was broken, it naturally turned into a support zone. The current price action shows a bearish candle with relatively high volume and a long wick. The wick attempts to sweep below the support area, but strong buying pressure pushes the price back up, allowing the candle to close well above the support zone. This is the first signal suggesting a potential reversal back into the uptrend.

Next, consider the angle of the corrective waves. We can identify two main pullback waves: C–D and E–F. It is easy to see that the E–F pullback is significantly flatter than the C–D pullback. This indicates that selling pressure has been gradually weakening up to the current candle.

These two factors support the bullish case within a strong uptrend. However, entering a trade at this moment would not offer an ideal reward–risk ratio because the pin bar has a long wick. Therefore, the better approach is to zoom into the chart and wait for a testing move that can shake out the final selling pressure before entering the trade.

Step 3: Trade Trigger

Figure 9.11: Example 5

Figure 9.11 presents the price action after the pin bar we analyzed earlier appeared. Let's examine the two bearish candles that follow that pin bar and see what the market is telling us.

I have aligned these two candles with their corresponding volume. Once again, we observe an imbalance between volume and spread. The second candle has higher volume than the first one. Under normal circumstances, this should reflect stronger selling pressure. However, the result is the opposite. The candle forms a classic E>R pattern—it has a very small body and even a long lower wick, indicating that the selling pressure has been significantly absorbed by buyers. According to our entry rules, we would normally wait for the third candle to appear—a bullish candle closing completely above the previous bearish candle. Conservative traders may choose to enter at the close of that candle, with a stop-loss placed below the final bearish candle and a take-profit at the nearest key resistance. Price reaches the profit target without much difficulty.

However, I chose an earlier entry, which illustrates the art of testing discussed in Chapter 6. From a testing perspective, the two candles we just examined represent the sellers' attempt to retest the key support zone. As we know, when candles test a support level with gradually weakening volume, it is a clear signal that sellers are running out of supply. Looking at the chart, both of these testing candles remain completely within the range of the previous pin bar, and their volume is significantly lower than that of the pin bar itself. This gives us enough confidence to enter a buy trade at the close of the final bearish candle in the pullback, without waiting for the next confirmation candle.

The entry, stop-loss, and take-profit levels are illustrated in Figure 9.11. As you can see, the art of analyzing testing allows us to achieve a better entry point and a significantly improved reward–risk ratio compared with waiting for a later confirmation entry.

Trade Example 6

In this final example, we turn to the stock market, examining the chart of Berkshire Hathaway on the 4-hour timeframe.

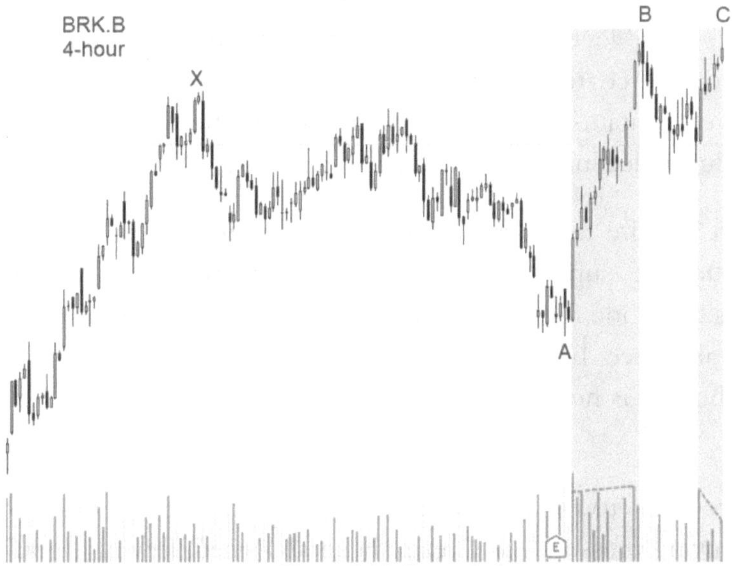

Figure 9.12: Example 6

Step 1: Analyze Market Structure

The market structure in this example is more complex, with both buyers and sellers showing strong participation. Both swing highs and swing lows on the chart have been broken. However, from a broader perspective, buyers still hold the advantage, as the swing high at B has broken above swing high X, which had remained intact for quite a long time before that. Meanwhile, A clearly serves as the swing low of this structure.

Step 2: Evaluate Momentum

Next, when evaluating market momentum, we observe that B and C are approaching price levels higher than X, forming two bullish waves with different volume characteristics. As shown in the figure, while the first bullish wave maintains consistently high volume, the second bullish wave shows gradually declining volume and remains at a relatively low level.

The reason is quite familiar: a strong historical resistance zone where a large amount of supply is concentrated (Figure 9.13). When price approaches this zone for the first time and forms peak B, buying pressure is quickly absorbed by the available supply. As a result, although the volume is high, it is not strong enough to push price above the resistance zone.

When price rises toward this area for the second time, much of the previous buying pressure has already been absorbed, leaving significantly less demand in the market. Consequently, the volume during this second attempt is noticeably lower than during the first one.

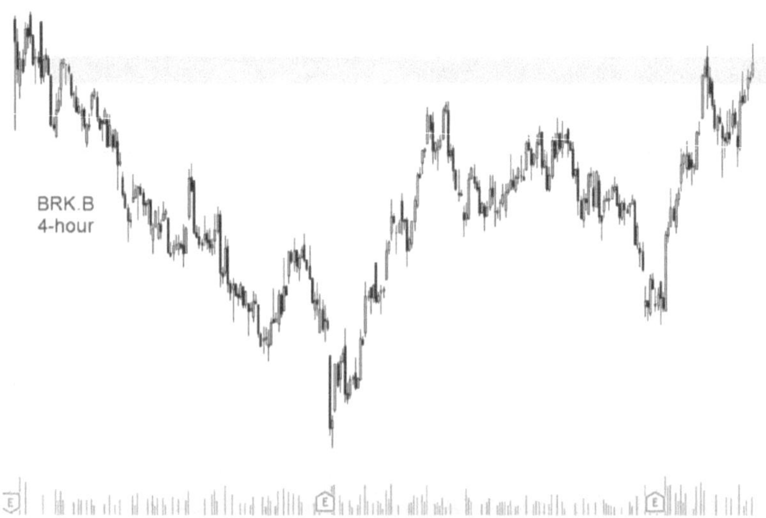

Figure 9.13: Example 6

Now, let's zoom out on the chart to analyze the candles together with their corresponding volume.

Figure 9.14: Example 6

Next, we assess the correlation between price and volume. We have two candles aligned with their corresponding volume as shown in Figure 9.14. In this two-candle pattern, the second candle has higher volume, but its body is only comparable to the previous candle while its upper wick is significantly longer, indicating rejection from sellers.

This is a classic case of high effort without a proportionate result (an E>R candle). It suggests that sellers are already present in this area and are suppressing the price. Therefore, no matter how strong the buying effort appears, it is not able to push the price much higher.

At this point, we need a third candle—the confirmation candle—to determine whether smart money is positioning on the buyer side or the seller side.

Step 3: Trade Trigger

Figure 9.15: Example 6

The third candle—the confirmation candle—closes near the lowest price of the previous candle, confirming that the bias of smart money is on the seller side. The subsequent bearish candles further reinforce the presence of smart money's position.

On the other hand, if you are a pure price action trader, you may identify this as a classic **double top pattern.** This double top is also confirmed by volume, which acts as a very strong confluence factor.

The entry, stop-loss, and take-profit levels are illustrated in the figure. If you apply the conservative take-profit approach (TP1), you would already achieve an R-R of 3, which is very impressive. If you are a trader following traditional price action methods with the double top pattern, you could target a further level at TP2. Alternatively, you could close 50% of the position at TP1, move the stop-loss to the entry point, and let the remaining 50% run toward TP2. Either way, this trade allows you to stack a decent amount of profit.

The trade example above is also the final example in this chapter. I hope the examples presented here have helped clarify how to trade with momentum in financial markets. This is one of the simplest yet most effective trading approaches, built upon the core principles of the market and focused on following the footprints of smart money. I hope you will apply the system shared in this book and practice it extensively to refine the three-step SMT trade trigger framework. The journey of learning through trading is never-ending—practice and backtest as much as possible so that SMT becomes your own SMT, tailored to your personal style and approach.

CHAPTER 10: THE TRADING ROADMAP TO MASTERY

You have now reached the final chapter of this book. However, this is not the end—this is where the real journey begins. The previous nine chapters have equipped you with a complete trading methodology through the SMT trading system. You now possess knowledge that most traders do not have. However, knowledge alone does not create successful traders. Consistent success only comes from applying that knowledge in real market conditions.

This chapter is designed to guide you from understanding the theory to mastering the practice. We will explore a structured training roadmap, the development of pattern recognition, common pitfalls traders face, essential resources, and several final pieces of guidance to help you begin your trading journey with confidence.

True mastery does not develop overnight. Professional traders often spend months, and even years, refining their skills before achieving consistent results. They do not rush the process and they do not take shortcuts. Instead, they follow a structured path of development. The roadmap presented in this chapter provides a systematic way to transform knowledge into practical skill. Each stage builds upon the previous one, and rushing through these stages often creates gaps in understanding. Those gaps eventually become weaknesses, and weaknesses frequently lead to losses in the market. For this reason, it is essential to follow the roadmap patiently and trust the process. With consistent effort and disciplined practice, the results will come.

Training Roadmap

Week 1–2: Master Market Structure

During the first two weeks, your focus should be entirely on market structure analysis. Open charts from different markets—stocks, forex, cryptocurrencies, or any other asset class. On each chart, mark the swing points using the five-candle rule. Determine the prevailing trend by identifying whether the market is moving upward, downward, or sideways. Then draw the key support and resistance zones and review the chart across multiple timeframes to confirm your analysis.

You should repeat this process on at least 50 different charts. During this phase, you should not place any trades and you should avoid overcomplicating the analysis. The goal is to practice pure structural analysis until it becomes intuitive. With enough repetition, you will gradually develop the ability to recognize market structure almost instantly. When you look at a chart, you should immediately see the trend direction, the major swing points, and the most important price zones.

At the beginning, analyzing a single chart may take five to seven minutes. By the end of the second week, the same analysis should take only twenty to thirty seconds. This increase in speed reflects growing familiarity and competence. Before moving forward, it is essential that your understanding of market structure becomes solid and reliable, because a strong structural foundation is required for every step that follows in the trading process.

Week 3–4: Add Momentum Analysis

During this phase, you return to the same 50 charts you analyzed earlier. The structural levels are already marked, so your task now is to layer momentum analysis on top of that foundation. Compare impulse waves with corrective waves, measure the distance between swings, and observe how volume evolves throughout each move. Pay close attention to whether the market is accelerating or decelerating.

For every chart you review, you should be able to answer a few key questions: Is the momentum strong, moderate, or weak? Does the momentum support the direction suggested by the market structure? At the beginning of this stage, combining structure and momentum analysis may take two to three minutes per chart. By the end of week four, that time should naturally decrease to around thirty to sixty seconds. At that point, the two analytical layers begin to operate almost automatically. You recognize the structure immediately, and you evaluate momentum almost instinctively. Your analytical foundation is now expanding and becoming more robust.

Week 5-6: Develop Pattern Recognition

At this stage, you move into one of the most important phases of the training process—developing the ability to recognize high-probability trading patterns. During these two weeks, analyze 100 new charts with a very specific objective: identifying the core setups of the SMT system.

Focus on locating testing patterns that occur with gradually declining volume. Practice identifying these patterns at multiple levels, including broader testing structures at the wave level as well as smaller testing formations within more localized price movements. At the same time, actively scan for E>R candles at key support and resistance zones—candles that display high volume but relatively small spread, indicating a mismatch between effort and result.

In addition, train yourself to recognize E<R candles as well. These candles display a large spread but relatively low volume, a pattern that often reflects the behavior of retail traders. Becoming familiar with these patterns will help you better understand market dynamics and avoid situations where retail activity may create misleading signals.

When a pattern appears, you should immediately verify several key factors. Confirm that the market structure aligns with the setup, evaluate whether the momentum supports the trade direction, check whether the volume confirms the signal, and assess whether the overall confluence is strong enough. This process ensures that every pattern is analyzed within the full SMT framework.

Whenever you identify a valid setup, capture a screenshot and organize it into categories. Record the context of the setup and its eventual outcome. Over time, this will build a valuable personal database of real market examples that strengthens your pattern recognition.

Each morning, quickly scan 10–15 charts to identify potential patterns and select three to five for deeper analysis. Each evening, review your observations and evaluate their accuracy so you can continuously learn from the market.

At first, patterns may appear unclear and you may feel uncertain about what you are seeing, which is completely normal. However, by the end of week six, patterns often begin to stand out clearly. You will start recognizing them almost instantly and noticing confirmation candles as they form. Your mindset gradually shifts from learning patterns to hunting patterns, and you begin approaching the market with trained eyes and growing confidence.

Week 7–8: Paper Trading with the Complete SMT System

During this phase, you begin applying the full SMT methodology in a live market environment using a demo account. The market is real and decisions are made in real time, but no actual capital is at risk. Your objective is to follow the SMT checklist with strict discipline. You should confirm that the market structure is clear, verify that momentum supports the setup, and ensure that every requirement of the system has been satisfied before executing a trade.

For each paper trade, record all relevant details, including the entry price, stop-loss level, profit targets, position size, and the reasoning behind the trade. You should then monitor the position, manage it according to your plan, take profits when appropriate, and accept losses when they occur.

At this stage, the goal is not to win every trade. The real objective is to execute the process consistently and correctly. In trading, disciplined execution matters far more than short-term results. By the end of week eight, the entire process should begin to feel natural and structured.

Week 9 and Beyond: Transition Gradually to Live Trading

After eight weeks of structured practice, you are ready to begin trading with real capital. However, you should start extremely small. Use micro positions and the minimum size allowed by your broker. At this stage, the goal is not to make profit but to experience the psychological pressure of trading with real money.

Trading psychology changes completely when actual capital is at risk. Paper trading is relatively easy, but live trading introduces emotional challenges. By keeping position sizes very small, you reduce financial risk while gaining valuable psychological experience.

You should continue trading with small size for at least 50 trades or three months, whichever period is longer. Once you have demonstrated consistency at this level—with a reasonable win rate, controlled losses, and stable emotional management—you can begin increasing your position size gradually. A practical approach is to increase your position size by about 25% after every 50 trades. This slow and disciplined progression helps prevent overconfidence and protects you from costly mistakes.

The structured training program requires approximately eight weeks of skill development before transitioning to live trading. During weeks 1–2, you focus on mastering market structure. In weeks 3–4, you add momentum analysis. Weeks 5–6 are dedicated to developing pattern recognition, and weeks 7–8 focus on paper trading with the complete SMT system. From week 9 onward, you begin trading with real capital using very small, micro-sized positions.

In total, the process typically requires at least three to four months. Many traders feel tempted to rush through this stage, but resisting that temptation is essential. Shortcuts in trading often lead to costly mistakes, while a properly built foundation supports long-term success. When the learning process is rushed, the foundation eventually collapses under market pressure. By contrast, patient and disciplined development creates the conditions for sustainable profitability. Trust the process, maintain your discipline, and continue progressing step by step toward mastery.

Pattern Recognition Skills

Pattern recognition is one of the key abilities that separates top traders from those who continue to struggle. Skilled traders can identify high-probability setups almost instantly, while struggling traders often miss opportunities or misinterpret the patterns that appear on the chart. The difference is not talent, but training.

Pattern recognition does not develop simply from reading books or studying theory. It develops through exposure—extensive exposure to real market examples. Traders improve this skill by reviewing hundreds of charts and repeating the same analytical process thousands of times. Through repetition, the brain gradually learns to recognize recurring market behaviors, and the neural pathways associated with these patterns become stronger with continued use.

Over time, this recognition process becomes increasingly automatic. Instead of consciously searching for patterns, experienced traders begin to notice them almost intuitively. The following section discusses practical ways to accelerate the development of this crucial pattern recognition ability.

Pattern Recognition Method #1: Retrospective Analysis

One of the most effective ways to develop pattern recognition is by studying completed market setups in historical charts. You scroll back through past price action and identify trading setups that have already played out. With the benefit of hindsight, the structure, momentum, and outcome of the setup become much clearer.

During this process, mark the entry point, the stop-loss level, and the profit targets that were eventually reached. Record the outcome of each example and organize these cases into a structured collection. Over time, you should aim to build a large library of historical examples, ideally containing at least 200 setups across the different SMT patterns.

By reviewing these examples repeatedly, your brain gradually absorbs the underlying patterns. The key characteristics become familiar, and the natural variations of each setup become easier to recognize. After studying more than 200 examples, these patterns begin to stand out clearly, even in the uncertainty of real-time market conditions.

Pattern Recognition Method #2: Real-Time Forward Testing

While retrospective analysis builds a strong pattern library, forward testing develops the ability to recognize setups under real-time uncertainty. Each morning, you scan a selection of charts and look for patterns that may be forming. When a potential setup appears, mark it on the chart and form a hypothesis about what might happen next.

Then you wait and observe. The pattern may complete successfully, or it may fail. Either outcome provides valuable feedback. If your identification is correct, your pattern library grows stronger. If it turns out to be incorrect, the lesson can be even more valuable because you learn what does **not** qualify as a valid pattern. Eliminating false positives is an essential part of developing trading judgment.

Forward testing strengthens your ability to distinguish between genuine setups and market noise. By repeating this exercise daily—spending about 30 to 60 minutes each morning—you gradually sharpen your pattern recognition. Over the course of several months, developing setups become easier to identify, and valid trading opportunities begin to stand out with much greater clarity.

Pattern Recognition Method #3: Detailed Journaling

Every trade deserves to be carefully documented. Capture a screenshot of the setup and annotate the chart. Record the structural context, your momentum assessment, the pattern you identified, and any confluence factors that supported the trade. You should also document the entry point, stop-loss level, profit targets, and the reasoning behind your decision.

Once the trade is closed, record the final outcome and note the lessons learned from the experience. At the end of each week, review your journal to identify recurring patterns in your behavior. This review process may reveal important questions: Are you frequently misidentifying certain setups? Are you entering trades too early or too late? Are you ignoring momentum signals or chasing trades that do not meet your criteria?

A trading journal often reveals truths that are difficult to see in the moment. By studying your records, you can adjust your approach and steadily improve your decision-making. Successful traders treat journaling as a disciplined habit, while unsuccessful traders often ignore it. In many cases, journaling becomes the key difference between traders who continuously learn and those who repeatedly make the same mistakes.

The three methods described above work most effectively when combined. Retrospective analysis helps you build a large pattern library, ideally consisting of at least 200 historical examples. Forward testing develops your ability to recognize patterns in real time, which can be practiced through a daily routine of 30–60 minutes of chart scanning. Detailed journaling then creates a feedback loop, allowing you to review your decisions and learn from them each week.

At that stage, trading gradually shifts from random speculation to a structured process of identifying and exploiting repeatable market patterns. For this reason, investing time in developing pattern recognition is one of the most valuable commitments a trader can make, because the long-term returns on that investment can be extraordinary.

Avoiding Common Pitfalls

This section outlines four of the most dangerous traps that frequently derail trading careers, along with practical strategies to avoid them. These pitfalls have the power to destroy trading accounts and discourage even the most motivated beginners. By recognizing them early and approaching the market with discipline, you can avoid many of the mistakes that prevent traders from achieving long-term success.

Trap #1: Chasing Every Setup

Many traders begin to see trading setups everywhere. Every pattern appears attractive, and every movement seems to present an opportunity. The result is excessive trading. Overtrading almost always leads to losses, as trading costs accumulate, mental fatigue increases, and decision quality begins to deteriorate. When attention is spread too thin, focus is lost and mistakes become more frequent.

A more effective approach is to become a specialist before trying to become a generalist. Choose one pattern that you understand well and focus on mastering it for the first three months. Develop deep familiarity with that setup and aim for consistent execution and a stable win rate. Once you have truly mastered one pattern, you can gradually add a second pattern and repeat the process.

Over time, your trading arsenal will expand naturally. However, during the early stages of development, depth of expertise is far more valuable than breadth. In trading, specialists consistently outperform generalists who attempt to trade everything at once.

Trap #2: Revenge Trading

Losses often trigger an emotional reaction. The mind naturally wants to recover what has been lost, and this desire can quickly push traders into abandoning their discipline. When revenge trading begins, traders ignore the SMT checklist, overlook the quality of the setup, and start forcing marginal trades that would normally be rejected. Many also increase their position size in an attempt to recover losses quickly, telling themselves that they "must win it back."

The outcome of this behavior is highly predictable. Losses usually grow larger, multiple losing trades accumulate, and the downward spiral accelerates. If this pattern continues unchecked, it can lead to severe account damage.

A practical solution is to implement a mandatory cooling-off rule. After any sequence of three consecutive losses, trading should stop for at least 24 hours. During this time, step away from the market completely. Clear your mind, review what happened objectively, and remind yourself that losses are a normal cost of doing business in trading.

Returning to the market with a calm and refreshed mindset allows rational analysis to replace emotional reaction. This type of forced break acts as a powerful psychological circuit breaker. When applied consistently, it protects both your trading account and your long-term trading career.

Trap #3: Overconfidence After a Winning Streak

After several consecutive winning trades, confidence can rise quickly. A trader who has just experienced five wins in a row may begin to feel invincible and believe that they have finally "figured out" the market. At this stage, risk management often starts to feel unnecessary. Position sizes increase, stop-loss levels are widened or removed entirely, and the trader convinces themselves that the next setup simply cannot fail.

Sooner or later, however, a losing trade appears—as it always does in trading. When that loss occurs with an oversized position and no proper stop-loss, the damage can be severe. A single catastrophic loss can erase the entire winning streak, damage the trading account, and shatter the trader's confidence.

The solution is simple but essential: treat every trade exactly the same. Winning streaks and losing streaks should never influence your risk management. Maintain the same level of risk per trade, follow the same checklist, and apply the same discipline every time you enter the market. The market does not care about your recent results, and it does not reward confidence alone. It rewards consistency.

Trap #4: Analysis Paralysis

As traders gain more knowledge, they also begin to notice more factors in the market. They analyze multiple timeframes, add more indicators, search for additional confluences, and consider an increasing number of variables before making a decision. While this deeper awareness may seem beneficial, it can easily lead to overanalysis. Traders begin waiting for the "perfect" setup, yet perfect setups rarely exist. As a result, opportunities are repeatedly missed, and frustration grows as the market moves without them.

The solution is to rely on a simple and disciplined decision framework. The SMT checklist already provides everything necessary for a trading decision. First, verify the market structure. Second, evaluate the momentum. Third, confirm that a valid setup is present. If these three elements align, the trade can be taken. If they do not align, the trade should be avoided.

This binary decision process removes unnecessary complexity. There is no need to evaluate dozens of additional factors or search endlessly for perfect conditions. The checklist prevents both overtrading and undertrading by providing a clear and consistent framework. By trusting this structure and executing decisions with confidence, traders can avoid the trap of analysis paralysis.

All of these traps originate from psychological weaknesses rather than technical limitations. Discipline is the tool that overcomes psychological pressure, and self-awareness makes discipline possible. You must continuously monitor your own behavior, recognize early warning signs of these traps, and apply the appropriate corrective actions immediately.

Never Stop Learning

The learning process does not end with this book. In trading, education is never truly complete because financial markets constantly evolve and trading techniques must adapt accordingly. Continuous learning is therefore essential for long-term success.

This section introduces several resources that can help you expand your knowledge beyond the SMT methodology. Trading communities can provide support, discussion, and shared experience, while various platforms offer valuable opportunities for practice and skill development.

However, it is important to use these resources wisely and maintain a healthy balance between learning and execution. Excessive studying can delay action, while taking action without continued learning often leads to repeating the same mistakes. The key is to maintain balance—continuing to learn while consistently applying what you have learned in practice.

Trading Communities

Trading can often feel isolating. Most traders work alone, without colleagues, casual conversations, or the daily interactions that exist in traditional workplaces. This isolation can easily lead to doubt and discouragement over time. A healthy trading community can provide valuable support, discussion, and perspective.

However, choosing the right community is essential. Many groups are filled with hype, unrealistic promises, and "get rich quick" narratives that ultimately harm developing traders. Instead, seek out communities where serious traders share thoughtful analysis, discuss setups objectively, and review trades in a constructive way.

Quality trading forums, Discord communities, trading-focused subreddits, and even local trading meetups can offer meaningful interaction with others who share similar goals. The key is to find a group that aligns with your methodology and encourages disciplined thinking.

At the same time, always maintain your independence as a trader. You must understand and take responsibility for every trade you place. Never follow someone else's ideas blindly. A community should support your learning process, but it should never replace your own analysis and judgment.

Practice Platforms

To make your learning curve truly effective, traders need a specialized tool, and my preferred platform for this purpose is Forex Tester Online. This platform allows traders to simulate real market conditions, build confidence, and refine their strategies before risking real capital.

Several features make it a leading solution for structured backtesting. The platform provides real tick-by-tick data, allowing traders to observe every price movement inside each candle rather than seeing only the completed candle. It also offers more than twenty years of historical market data, enabling traders to test strategies across bull markets, bear markets, and sideways conditions.

Because it runs directly in the browser, the platform can be accessed from virtually any device without complicated installation. It also includes advanced position management tools that allow traders to jump instantly to take-profit or stop-loss outcomes and adjust the simulation speed to accelerate the learning process. Detailed performance analytics help traders evaluate strengths and weaknesses in their execution.

Additional features include the ability to import trades from MT4 or MT5, as well as the option to simulate prop-firm challenges with strict rules such as maximum drawdown limits and daily loss restrictions. With this platform, traders can backtest not only the SMT system but virtually any trading methodology, at any time and from anywhere.

You can explore this excellent tool here: frankmillertrading.com/backtest.

The Real Journey Begins

We are approaching the end of this book after ten chapters that together present a complete trading methodology. However, it is essential to remember a fundamental truth: trading is a marathon rather than a sprint.

True success in trading cannot be judged by a single trade, a single week, or even a single month. Instead, it is measured through consistent performance maintained over many years, often across decades, and sometimes across an entire lifetime of market participation.

The SMT methodology provides a genuine trading edge. An edge does not guarantee that every trade will be profitable, but it does shift probabilities in the trader's favor. In practice, a win rate of around 55–60% is achievable. When this win rate is combined with a risk-reward ratio of approximately 2:1, the long-term mathematics of trading become favorable. The advantage may appear modest, but it is sufficient when applied consistently. Over time, profits accumulate, compound, and grow steadily. Applying a modest edge consistently for twenty years can create significant wealth, while expecting miracles within two months almost always leads to disappointment. Realistic expectations are therefore essential. The SMT methodology is powerful, but it is not magic. Understanding this distinction allows traders to approach the market with clarity and patience, which ultimately supports consistent profitability.

This book provides a roadmap for your journey. A roadmap can show the destination, the obstacles along the way, and the path that connects them, yet it cannot walk the path on your behalf. Each trader must move forward step by step, face challenges, and continue progressing through effort and persistence. No one can hand you trading success, because success must be earned through dedication, practice, and resilience. Along the way there will be failures, lessons, moments of frustration, and periods of growth. These experiences are part of the transformation that turns a beginner into a capable trader. The journey is demanding, but it is also deeply rewarding for those who remain committed. The most important step is to begin the journey today.

Before you begin the next chapter of your trading journey, may I ask one small favor?

CHANGE LIVES WITH YOUR REVIEW

Every trader's journey is different, but one thing is always true: we all learn faster when someone shares what they've discovered.

If this book helped you understand momentum more clearly, improve your market analysis, or simply look at price action from a new perspective, I would be grateful if you shared your experience with a quick, honest review.

Many traders spend years trying to connect market structure, volume, and momentum into one complete picture. Your review could help someone discover that missing piece much sooner.

Reviews don't just support authors—they help fellow traders decide which resources are worth their time and attention.

To leave your review, simply scan the QR code below:

Thank you for taking a moment to support both this book and the trading community.

Frank Miller

CHECK OUT OTHER BOOKS

Scan this barcode to access my full collection of trading books-packed with proven methods, fresh insights, and powerful techniques to help you trade smarter and grow faster.	
Scan this barcode to stay updated when new books are released.	

Made in United States
Troutdale, OR
08/13/2026

52845072R00110